Contents

The way, truth and life...

Happy Easter! That joy, that truth, that resurrected life – it isn't just for chocolate egg season, but, as Cath Butler highlights, *continues* from what has been, is now and will be in the future. We are always an Easter people, empowered by God's Spirit, who look ahead to our coming King!

As we dig into the Bible, we discover it's *all* about Jesus. Richard Ellwood leads us through the Easter story in Luke. Here, we see Jesus at the centre of God's story, making sense of what has been and what is to come. We may have struggled with Old Testament law (see this issue's Spotlight), but Phil Winn gently unpacks chapters from Leviticus with its theme of what it means to be a holy people living before a holy God. Praise God for our Saviour! His sacrifice alone has rescued us and made us holy.

That Old Testament story continues through kings like David and Solomon (1 Kings), through harsh times of disobedience, oppression and restitution. Finally, there is rebirth of God's people as the church – a new era of which we are part. Like that early church in Crete (Titus), we wrestle with issues of truth. Like the early church in Acts, there are issues of conflict inside and opposition from without. Through it all, God's Spirit shapes us, leading us to growth in Christ, as we receive and share his life.

Still, now, as we listen and hear his Word, Jesus comes and stands among us and says: 'Peace be with you' (Luke 24:36).

'Tricia and Emlyn Williams
Editors

Daily Bread toolbox

...cia & Emlyn
...liams

...ked with
...pture Union
...many years.
...lyn led Schools
...istry, then
...ked with SU
...ernational.
...cia was also
...t of the
...ools team
...d later worked
...SU Publishing,
...veloping,
...ting and
...ting Bible
...ources.
...ving recently
...npleted
...earch in the
...a of faith
...d dementia,
...e continues
...h writing and
...ting faith
...ources. Retired
...m his role
...discipleship
...stor in a local
...urch, Emlyn
...w continues
...writing and
...king-with-
...ople ministries.

WAY IN

This page introduces both the notes and the writer. It sets the scene and tells you what you need to know to get into each series.

A DAY'S NOTE

The notes for each day include five key elements: *Prepare, Read* (the Bible passage for the day), *Explore, Respond* and *Bible in a year*. These are intended to provide a helpful way of meeting God in his Word.

PREPARE

Prepare yourself to meet with God and pray that the Holy Spirit will help you to understand and respond to what you read.

READ

Read the Bible passage, taking time to absorb and simply enjoy it. A verse or two from the Bible text is usually included on each page, but it's important to read the whole passage.

EXPLORE

Explore the meaning of the passage, listening for what God may be saying to you. Before you read the comment, ask yourself: what is the main point of this passage? What is God showing me about himself or about my life? Is there a promise or a command, a warning or example to take special notice of?

RESPOND

Respond to what God has shown you in the passage in worship and pray for yourself and others. Decide how to share your discoveries with others.

BIBLE IN A YEAR

If your aim is to know God and his Word more deeply, why not follow this plan and read the whole Bible in one year?

Small can be significant

A group of five small rural churches, not a church hall between them, is not the likeliest setting for flourishing outreach. But with your support and much prayer, they are reaching out to young people in their community. And there's a strong sense that God is at work.

SU Mission Enabler Lisa Jones was sharing our Revealing Jesus mission framework at Rochester Diocese in March 2021. It was there that she met Becky Parnham. Becky is the Children and Families worker for the five churches forming the united benefice of Coxheath, East Farleigh, Linton, Hunton and West Farleigh, based in the Kentish countryside to the south-east of Maidstone.

Lisa says, 'Becky told me they had a few children who came to church, although not regularly. They also ran a toddler group and an after-school club for Key Stage 2 children. She was excited about the Revealing Jesus framework and wanted SU's help to do more to connect with children in the wider community.

So I arranged to train her and five volunteers from across the churches as Faith Guides, and support them to get things going.'

Finding ways round the challenges

There were some issues to overcome. Lisa says, 'All of the churches are old buildings. One even has box pews! None of the churches has a hall and only one has wi-fi. The congregations are all very small and they were between vicars too. It was important that they were realistic about what they could manage to do.

'On the plus side, Becky and the team realised that they were not making the best of what each church could offer, and all of them were very different. We worked through the challenges, identified what skills and availability each volunteer had, and came up with a manageable plan.'

Holy Trinity: An after-school haven

Holy Trinity Church in Coxheath is a former workhouse chapel, very small with narrow pews. But it is right in the centre of a village that has doubled in size over the past ten years. Becky says, 'We have nearly 4,000 residents now, and incoming families in particular really welcome the opportunity to connect with one another and build social links. Holy Trinity, based close to the school, is perfectly placed to be at the heart of that.

'We developed "Crafternoon", offering children craft activities based on a theme. The first one was held in

the autumn around Halloween, so our theme was Jesus as light of the world. We offered refreshments and a reflection at the end.

'Families just flooded in, and kept coming...'

'I told the mums at our toddler group about it; we posted on social media and we thought perhaps 30 people might turn up. Right before the event, we committed it to God in prayer – we felt that was really important. Then we opened the doors.

'Families just flooded in, and kept coming, over 90 adults and children in all! Somehow the crafts and refreshments stretched! We chatted with parents and children and there was a real buzz. It was a great way to get our connections with the community going again after the Covid lockdown. Afterwards, one of the mums posting on Facebook summed it up as "Amazing craft, cake, welcome, atmosphere – just fab! Thank you!" Another parent said, "I can imagine the effort you all went to, it was just brilliant! Lots of engaging and fun activities, I've come home with lots to go in the fridge!"'

Becky says, 'We've continued to offer Crafternoons because they are so popular. We're also hoping to start a weekly after-school drop-in for older children, a safe space with games and a tuck shop. We'll involve the young people in deciding what to include so it meets their needs.'

SU article

St Nicholas: Muddy Church

The idyllic village of Linton is a tenth of the size of Coxheath. Set on a hill in a conservation area, it has far-reaching views across the Kentish Weald. The thirteenth-century church of St Nicholas in the middle of the village has beautiful grounds, a large car park and is on a popular walking route.

Becky says, 'We felt that families in the area would be interested in nature, so in November 2021 we tried out having a 'Muddy Church' event, with a nature-themed trail for families to follow. We gave them a booklet with questions they could discover the answers to as they walked around the church grounds.

'Our little church team built a campfire and, once the families had completed their walk, we invited them to come and share hot drinks and snacks with us and enjoy the warmth and camaraderie. It gave us the opportunity to make connections and chat, and for them to reflect on what they had enjoyed about the trail.

'Because the church is on a walking route, we left the trail up and used posters to promote it so that families who weren't at the event could still visit and do the trail in their own time. Since then, we've had events and introduced new trail themes every couple of months.

'Our prayer is that the relationships we are building with the families will develop and that eventually this will become more of a Grow Community.'

A spiritual harvest in the making

Becky can really see the value of using SU's Revealing Jesus mission framework to underpin outreach work and help develop activities for each church based on the mission stage they are at. It's also helped her bring others in the church on the journey as they now understand the framework too.

There's a sense of anticipation right across the churches. 'We all feel that God's doing something significant here, as if there's an undercurrent of energy bubbling up under the surface,' Becky says. 'There's the opportunity for a big harvest. At the moment there aren't many of us to reap it. But with Lisa's support, and through committing all our plans to God in prayer, I believe that anything is possible.'

A shorter version of this story first appeared in Connecting You, *SU's free quarterly supporter magazine. If you'd like to receive copies of* Connecting You *and learn more of how God is moving in the hearts and lives of children and young people today, you can sign up online at su.org.uk/connectingyou.*

At Scripture Union, we're passionate about helping churches to connect with non-church children and young people in the wider community. To find out more about the Revealing Jesus mission framework, and how SU can support your church in mission, visit su.org.uk/revealingjesus

Before I leave you

About the writer
Jennie Pollock

Jennie is Head of Public Policy at the Christian Medical Fellowship, and a writer and editor. Her first book, on contentment, is available now. She lives, works and worships in central London, blogs at jenniepollock.com and tweets as @missjenniep

Jesus' triumphal entry to Jerusalem marked the beginning of the final week before his arrest and crucifixion. As we read through these chapters, it becomes clear that Jesus knows his time on earth is coming to an end and wants to make sure he says everything he needs to. He starts to make more provocative statements to the religious leaders. He spends a lot of time in the Temple courts, teaching and preaching the gospel. And he gives his followers hints about the persecutions to come, along with instructions about how to face them.

But first, we will see him demonstrating exactly what kind of king he is: the kind that comes humbly, riding the foal of a donkey.

We will get an insight into his heart, too, which will help set the context for some of the harsh things he says to the scribes, Pharisees and teachers of the law: he weeps over Jerusalem.

For hundreds of years this city, with its glorious Temple in the centre, had been the place on earth where God's presence was most tangibly manifested. Yet when the Son of the King came to it, this royal city would completely fail to recognise him. Or perhaps, as we will see in the parable of the vineyard, those who should have been most eagerly awaiting him *would* recognise him and would knowingly turn against him.

No wonder he wept.

Saturday 1 April
Luke 22:24–38

A kingdom of servants

PREPARE
Think of believers you know or have known who serve the church in love and humility. Thank the Lord for them. Ask him to help you put to death any pride or self-seeking in your heart.

....

READ
Luke 22:24–38

EXPLORE
How easily we slip from moments of great depth, significance and worship into our old, sinful patterns! It is likely that the disciples were still sitting at the meal table – with the taste of the precious symbols of Jesus' coming sacrifice still on their lips – when they started arguing about which of them was the greatest (v 24).

Jesus taught them, again, that his kingdom is not like the kingdoms of the world. Yes, he would make the disciples great, but they weren't to exploit this, rather to act as willing servants. The way of love described in 1 Corinthians 13:4–7 provides a good picture of the kind of leadership they should have embodied.

Notice also the promise of restoration in verses 31 and 32. Jesus knew that all the disciples would be tested, and Peter in particular would fail the test. Yet he also knew that Peter would repent. He would 'turn back' (v 32) – and when he did, he was to strengthen the others.

What a gracious, glorious Lord – even before we fail him, he is ready to forgive and to use us again!

> 'And I confer on you a kingdom, just as my Father conferred one on me.'
> **Luke 22:29**

RESPOND
Thank the Lord for his patience with you, and his unending forgiveness for your sins and failures. Thank him that he knows all about you, loves you and even prays for you.

....

Bible in a year: Joshua 1–3; Psalm 37

Join the joyful procession

PREPARE
On the first Palm Sunday, the crowds sang Psalm 118:26 in praise to Jesus. One day we will sing it again as he returns in glory!

....

READ
Psalm 118

EXPLORE
When we feel great joy, we often express it physically. Football supporters hug one another and jump up and down when they score a goal. Audiences stand, clap and stamp their feet after an excellent performance. In some countries drivers toot their horns whenever they pass a wedding. And in Israel, people celebrated by waving palm branches.

Some church traditions have lost this physical expression of praise, preferring to be more 'decorous'. The nineteenth-century preacher CH Spurgeon bemoaned this 'excessive propriety'.* To him, 'a little sacred excess' seemed a more appropriate response to the kinds of things we see listed in this psalm: God's presence, his help, his deliverance, his victory, his salvation and, of course, his enduring love.

This love marks God out from all other rulers and idols. In love he created us.

In his love he sent his Son to die for us (John 3:16). In love he abides with us, disciplines us, strengthens us and helps us. His love never fails (1 Corinthians 13:8).

Whatever is happening in your life, you can be assured that God's love for you endures for ever.

Blessed is he who comes in the name of the LORD. From the house of the LORD we bless you.
Psalm 118:26

RESPOND
We have so much to thank God for. Use this psalm to inspire you to list some of the ways he has helped you, blessed you and sustained you. And when you feel the joy welling up, let it show!

*CH Spurgeon, *Spurgeon on the Psalms*, Destiny Image Publishers, 2015

....

Bible in a year: Joshua 4,5; Romans 10

WAY IN
Luke 22–24

It's all about Jesus

About the writer
Richard Ellwood

After several years pastoring an international French-speaking church in Brussels, Belgium, Richard has recently returned to the UK. He lives with his wife and family in Oxfordshire, where they serve their local church.

The Bible is a collection of books written by a multitude of different authors spanning many centuries. Books of wisdom and poetry find their place alongside stories of prophets, priests and kings. Detailed legal stipulations precede brutal tales of war. Wild apocalyptic prophecies follow carefully constructed letters. It is an eclectic mix. Is it, however, a mix with any coherent semblance of unity?

From reading the final chapters of the Gospel of Luke, the answer must surely be a resounding 'Yes!' As we read these chapters, we are taken to the central point of the whole of the Bible: the death and resurrection of Jesus Christ. Luke recounts in detail the physical, emotional and psychological pain Jesus suffered in the hours leading up to his death before recording the glory and power of the resurrection. It is his description of Jesus' explanation for the events of our readings which leaves little room for doubt as to what, or who, the Bible is all about: 'And beginning with Moses and all the Prophets, he explained to them what was said in all the Scriptures concerning himself' (Luke 24:27).

Like a series of streams all leading back to the same source, the books of the Bible are all about Jesus. Easter is all about Jesus. As we read these familiar, yet enduringly powerful stories which close Luke's Gospel, the challenge is to ensure our lives are all about Jesus too.

The perfect will of God

PREPARE
Have you ever messed up? You're in good company!

....

READ
Luke 22:39–53

EXPLORE
We can all find it hard to stay awake sometimes, whether it be in front of the TV, after lunch on Christmas Day or during the Sunday sermon! This can be embarrassing or inconvenient, but in today's passage we see the disciples falling asleep during a prayer time hours before Jesus' death. What shame they must have felt! It is, however, only the first of three examples in this passage of Jesus' disciples messing up and disappointing him. After the disciples struggling to stay awake (v 45) we read of Judas' betrayal of Jesus (v 47) before another disciple violently attacks a servant (v 50). Luke diplomatically leaves out the identity of the angry disciple, but John tells us it is Peter (see John 18:10).

Three acts of human frailty and sinfulness: the physical tiredness of the sleeping disciples; the hypocrisy and cowardice of Judas; and the angry revenge and violence shown by Peter.

These three acts are in stark contrast to Jesus' powerful and sacrificial submission to the will of his Father which precedes them: 'not my will, but yours be done' (v 42). The disciples had their will and agenda, whereas Jesus submitted his will and agenda to his heavenly Father.

> 'Father, if you are willing, take this cup from me; yet not my will, but yours be done.'
>
> **Luke 22:42**

RESPOND
We are all sinful individuals who mess up from time to time as we pursue our will rather than God's. Thank God today for his kindness in forgiving your mistakes and submit afresh to the will of God the Father.

....

Bible in a year: Joshua 6,7; Romans 11

Tuesday 4 April
Luke 22:54–71

Responding to injustice

PREPARE

Have you ever been let down by a friend or unjustly treated at work? How should we respond to injustice?

· ·

READ

Luke 22:54–71

EXPLORE

When They See Us is a 2019 Netflix series telling the story of five black teenagers from Harlem, unjustly convicted for a murder they did not commit. The series has been streamed millions of times and received multiple awards. It is, however, a hard watch. Injustice is always hard to watch, and even harder to experience. In today's passage, Jesus is the recipient of terrible injustices from people who were supposed to love and protect him. He is denied by one of his closest disciples (vs 54–62) and mocked, blindfolded and beaten by guards (vs 63–65) before being condemned by the religious authorities of the day (vs 66–71). Peter's sin is cowardice; the guards' and the leaders' cruelty, an abuse of power.

What is Jesus' response to such sinful injustice? He is largely quiet and submissive, but his words also point to the bigger picture: 'from now on, the Son of Man will be seated at the right hand of the mighty God' (v 69). Jesus sees that these injustices are not the end of the story – they are even, in part, necessary for God's great plan of salvation to be realised. He sees that following his death and resurrection will be his ascension to heaven where he will reign at the right hand of God.

> The Lord turned and looked straight at Peter. Then Peter remembered the word the Lord had spoken to him: 'Before the cock crows today, you will disown me three times.'
> **Luke 22:61**

RESPOND

If you are experiencing injustice right now, ask God to help you see the bigger picture of his purposes in your life.

· ·

Bible in a year: Joshua 8,9; Romans 12

True authority

PREPARE
As you read of the suffering and injustice Jesus endured on his way to the cross, let God speak to you afresh about the enormity of Jesus' actions in these tumultuous hours before his death.

READ
Luke 23:1–12

EXPLORE
Are you in a position of authority? In your family, workplace or church? Authority is a powerful thing to hold. Sometimes it is earned, sometimes given freely, sometimes seized. It is often abused, misunderstood and resisted. Yet, true authority when rightly used can be liberating and inspiring.

In today's passage we see terrible examples of authority being used for selfish, corrupt and ultimately evil purposes. The religious authorities continue hounding Jesus, fabricating a political charge against him to justify taking him to Pilate (vs 1,2). Pilate himself, the secular governor of Judea, seeks to pass on the authority he has received by sending Jesus to Herod (vs 6,7). Pilate hopes Herod can take the difficult decision out of his hands, but Herod – a man oozing authority and corruption in equal measure – simply mocks and ridicules Jesus before returning him to Pilate.

In the midst of all this, much like in our reading yesterday, Luke shows Jesus as the one person who had true, authentic authority. He is once again submissive to the will and authority of his heavenly Father as he allows the events to unfold.

So Pilate asked Jesus, 'Are you the king of the Jews?' 'You have said so,' Jesus replied.

Luke 23:3

RESPOND
How do you handle the authority you carry? With humility and servant-heartedness? Or with selfishness and pride? Ask God to help you lead and exercise authority in a way that honours God and serves people.

Bible in a year: Joshua 10,11; Psalm 38

Thursday 6 April
Luke 23:13–25

The ultimate substitution

PREPARE
What would you have done in Pilate's position? Sought a compromise, stood up to the crowd or succumbed to their wishes?

....

READ
Luke 23:13–25

EXPLORE
We are all used to the concept of a substitute. Football teams take off an injured player and replace him or her with a substitute. Schools use substitute teachers to fill staffing needs. When cooking we sometimes substitute certain ingredients for others because of dietary requirements or convenience. One person or object takes the place of another.

In our reading today, we read of a substitution like no other as Barabbas is spared death and Jesus takes his place. Luke is at pains to point out the differences between these two men. Pilate says he finds no basis for the charges brought against Jesus before stating simply, 'he has done nothing to deserve death' (v 15). This is in stark contrast to Barabbas who has been convicted of insurrection and murder (v 19). The one who is guilty of taking life will have his life spared while the other – 'the author of life' (Acts 3:15) – will be killed in his place.

Most of us have not murdered or caused a riot. Most of us may not have a criminal record. And yet, as the apostle Paul writes, 'all have sinned and fall short of the glory of God' (Romans 3:23). Jesus, the ultimate substitute, chose to die in our place. As Barabbas walked free, so do we.

So Pilate decided to grant their demand. He released the man who had been thrown into prison for insurrection and murder, the one they asked for, and surrendered Jesus to their will.
Luke 23:24,25

RESPOND
Thank God for the great substitution that took place when Jesus died in our place.

....

Bible in a year: Joshua 12–15; Romans 13

Words from the heart

PREPARE
On this Good Friday ask God to speak to you in a fresh way as you read the familiar story of Jesus on the cross.

● ●

READ
Luke 23:26–43

EXPLORE
We're taught from early childhood that our words matter. But what comes out of our *mouths* has its origin elsewhere. Earlier in his Gospel, Luke shows Jesus teaching about the link between our mouth and our heart: 'For the mouth speaks what the heart is full of' (Luke 6:45). Here, the cruelty of the previous hours continues as Jesus is mocked and insulted. Until now Jesus has offered few words, often remaining silent to the frustration of those trying to send him to his death. Now, though, as we arrive at the most painful moment of Jesus' life on earth, Jesus does speak – and his heart is revealed.

He first summons energy to speak to the women mourning for him (vs 28–30). It is men who have dominated this story, and yet it is women that Jesus first addresses on his way to the cross. He then speaks to God the Father, asking him to forgive his persecutors (v 34), before granting the gift of eternal life to the repentant criminal (v 43).

Giving dignity to women, asking forgiveness of his killers and promising eternal life to a convicted criminal: these are the priorities of Jesus' heart, which are spoken by his mouth at his greatest time of trial.

'Father, forgive them, for they do not know what they are doing.'
Luke 23:34

RESPOND
Take time today to reflect on the state of your own heart. Do your words reveal a heart in need of God's care and correction?

● ●

Bible in a year: Joshua 16–19; Romans 14

Saturday 8 April
Luke 23:44–56

Jesus' final words

PREPARE
How easy do you find it to submit to God's will for your life?

. . . .

READ
Luke 23:44–56

EXPLORE
Yesterday we read the words Jesus uttered on the final leg of his journey to death. We read of how he gave dignity and forgiveness to those around him. Today we read of the very last words he spoke before 'he breathed his last' (v 46). We are often intrigued to know people's last words before they die. We hope they can somehow comfort us in grief as well as give an insight into the individual. This is certainly the case in the final words of Jesus.

These eight words of Jesus sum up his attitude to the mission given to him by God; a mission which began in the simplicity of a stable: 'Father, into your hands I commit my spirit' (v 46). In words which echo another eight-word prayer he prayed only a few hours earlier in the garden of Gethsemane ('yet not my will, but yours be done', Luke 22:42), Jesus submits to the plans God has for his life and ministry even while experiencing exhaustion, humiliation and agony.

Today, as we sit between the pain of Good Friday and the joy of Easter Sunday, we are confronted again with the humbling fact that it is Jesus' submission that brought us freedom; his humility that brought us new life with God the Father.

'Father, into your hands I commit my spirit.'
Luke 23:46

RESPOND
'Lord Jesus, I thank you afresh for your submission to the will and mission of your Father. Help me in turn to live in joyful submission to your will for my life.'

. . . .

Bible in a year: Joshua 20–22; Psalm 39

He is risen!

PREPARE
Happy Easter! Begin today by thanking God for the gift of life which is possible thanks to the resurrection of Jesus.

READ
Luke 24:1–12

EXPLORE
Millions of Christians around the world today are celebrating the simple but majestic content of today's reading – that Jesus is alive! We have focused much on the words of Jesus in the final hours before his death. In today's story, although Jesus is absent from the scene, his words are still present and, like his words of the previous days, much is revealed to us through them. To the fear, sadness, disappointment and confusion the women must have felt, shock is added as they encounter not only an empty tomb but two angels who 'gleamed like lightning' (v 4). What follows, however, are the words of Jesus quoted by the angels who urge the women to 'remember how he told you' that he would 'be crucified and on the third day be raised again' (vs 6,7). His words offer the proof of his authority: what he said would happen has happened.

The resurrection shows once and for all that Jesus carries true power and authority and, ultimately, that what he says is true. Easter tells us that you and I can trust Jesus with our lives and that he will not let us down. He has embraced death and he has, as he said he would, come out the other side alive and victorious.

'Why do you look for the living among the dead? He is not here; he has risen!'
Luke 24:5,6

RESPOND
Do you find it easy to trust God? How does the reality of the resurrection affect this?

Bible in a year: Joshua 23,24; Romans 15

Monday 10 April
Luke 24:13–35

Sharing your faith

PREPARE
When did you last share your faith with a non-Christian?

. . . .

READ
Luke 24:13–35

EXPLORE
How easy do you find it to talk to others about Jesus? Does the word 'evangelism' strike fear into your heart? Or do you jump at the chance to share your faith with your friends?

As Luke starts to conclude his account of the life and ministry of Jesus, he offers us Jesus' way of talking to others about faith. We see Jesus walking with two despondent disciples, asking them questions and listening. It seems Jesus wants to give these men space to speak and share their hearts. When the time comes, however, Jesus moves the conversation on, and 'beginning with Moses and all the Prophets' (v 27) he explains how the story of the Bible leads up to him and the amazing events of the previous days. Food and prayer play their part too as the two men are drawn into a fresh understanding of the identity of Jesus over a meal.

What a great example for us as we think about sharing our faith with others. Following Jesus' example, God calls us to walk closely with those around us, being willing to ask relevant questions and listen carefully. We can share life around meal tables and not be afraid to pray for people as needs arise. Then at the appropriate time, under the leading of the Holy Spirit, we can explain how Jesus fits into the big story of life.

And beginning with Moses and all the Prophets, he explained to them what was said in all the Scriptures concerning himself.

Luke 24:27

RESPOND
Who can you walk with and share the story of Jesus with this week?

. . . .

Bible in a year: Judges 1,2; Romans 16

Peace and joy

PREPARE
Take time to look back over the readings from Luke over the past few days. What has struck you the most and what is God highlighting to you at this time?

READ
Luke 24:36–53

EXPLORE
We all love it when a story ends well! Whether it's the princess finding her prince, the underdog becoming the hero or the mystery being solved. Not only does Luke's Gospel finish with a happy ending, it also closes in a way which mirrors its opening. At the beginning of the book angels announced that with the birth of Jesus comes the promise of peace and joy to all (Luke 2:10–14). Now, as we reach the end of the Gospel, we read the same two words. After a traumatic few days, Jesus extends 'peace' to the 'startled and frightened' disciples (vs 36,37) before they return to Jerusalem, not in grief but 'with great joy' (v 52).

By his death Jesus has brought peace to us all. We can now be at peace with God the Father who accepts the sacrificial death of his Son in our place. And there can be no better thing than being at peace with our Creator God! It is, therefore, entirely appropriate for peace to be accompanied by joy.

Peace and joy bookend today's passage as well as the whole of Luke's Gospel, but they are also meant to be the defining characteristics of those who follow Jesus.

> While they were still talking about this, Jesus himself stood among them and said to them, 'Peace be with you.'
> **Luke 24:36**

RESPOND
Ask the Holy Spirit to fill you with peace and joy today as you seek to be a disciple of Jesus.

Bible in a year: Judges 3,4; Mark 1

Scripture Union
holidays

Amazing Christian holidays

for **children & young people**

FIND OUT MORE
su.org.uk/ holidays

Holy God, holy people

Leviticus has a reputation for being a difficult book, full of obscure rules and regulations. Does it have anything to teach us as Christians in the twenty-first century? Although our circumstances may be very different, we serve the

same God. Look behind the outward appearance at the principles and we can learn much about living in relationship to God.

Rescued from slavery in Egypt, the people of God are led through the wilderness towards the Promised Land. God travels with them, and will be with them in their new homeland, but how can the Holy One live among unholy people? God calls his people to be holy, as he is holy; that means that they are separated out for him and are to be distinctive.

God had instructed Moses to build a portable worship area, the tabernacle. At its heart was the tent of meeting, which contained the Most Holy Place, which contained the Ark of the Covenant, and, outside that, the Holy Place. For details of the tabernacle see chapters 25–27 of Exodus. Artistic representations can be found in many illustrated Bibles and reference books or on the Internet.

The concept of 'clean' is introduced earlier in Leviticus. Only clean things and clean people can come into God's presence. Becoming unclean is unavoidable, but cleansing is available and should be used before approaching the Lord.

As Christians, indwelt by God's Holy Spirit, how do we live holy lives in the world today? Leviticus gives us some guiding principles.

About the writer
Phil Winn

After working in schools, churches and hospitals, Phil has retired to Sheffield where, as a schoolboy, he was introduced to *Daily Bread*. He and his wife, Pauline, enjoy spending time with their family and exploring the beautiful Peak District.

Wednesday 12 April
Leviticus 16:1–34

A tale of two goats

PREPARE
Meditate on 1 John 1:9. 'If we confess our sins, he is faithful and just and will forgive us our sins and purify us from all unrighteousness.'

. . . .

READ:
Leviticus 16:1–34

EXPLORE
Visiting Manchester Art Gallery, I was struck by a painting of a goat, looking sorry for itself, alone in a wilderness. It was *The Scapegoat* by William Holman Hunt,* the second of the goats used in the Day of Atonement.

How could a holy God live among a people who repeatedly sinned and fell short of his standards? This was the only day of the year when the priest could enter the Most Holy Place, the inner part of the tent of meeting where the Ark of the Lord was. He did so to sprinkle blood from a bull (sacrificed as his own sin offering) and from the first goat (a sin offering for the people), before doing the same in the tent of meeting. In this way the people's sin is atoned for and the pollution of the people's sin is removed from the place where God lives among them.

Sacrifices were made regularly, but on this day, an additional ceremony was enacted as the priest confessed the people's sins over the goat before sending it into the wilderness (v 21). What a striking illustration of the removal of sin.

In Jesus we see both the atoning sacrifice (Romans 3:25) and the one who bears away our sin (1 Peter 2:24).

'The goat chosen by lot as the scapegoat shall be presented alive before the Lord to be used for making atonement by sending it into the wilderness as a scapegoat.'
Leviticus 16:10

RESPOND
Thank God that 'as far as the east is from the west, so far has he removed our transgressions from us' (Psalm 103:12).

*https://en.wikipedia.org/wiki/The_Scapegoat_(painting)

. . . .

Bible in a year: Judges 5,6; Psalms 40,41

Washed in the blood

PREPARE
'Let us draw near to God with a sincere heart and with the full assurance that faith brings' (Hebrews 10:22).

. . . .

READ
Leviticus 17:1–16

EXPLORE
The restrictions on making sacrifices in the first part of the chapter are understandable. If individuals made their own sacrifices, it would be easy for offerings to the Lord to be confused with the sacrifices surrounding peoples made to their own gods. Soon the Lord's people would be worshipping false gods. Limiting the ways in which sacrifice could be made ensured the purity of worship.

The ban on the consumption of blood and the strict instructions on slaughtering animals for meat may seem less obvious. Blood, however, was central to the sacrificial system. Essential to life, it was used as a symbol of purification in the Day of Atonement (v 11). When an animal was slaughtered for meat, it had to be done in such a way that the blood was drained from it, so that no one would consume it (v 14b).

Imagine the shock of observant Jews, brought up on this teaching, when Jesus said, 'Unless you eat the flesh of the Son of Man and drink his blood, you have no life in you' (John 6:53). The blood of animals, never a permanent solution to sin, pointed to Jesus' sacrifice (see Hebrews 10:4). Symbolised by the shedding of his blood, to 'drink his blood' meant to appropriate for oneself the benefits of his sacrifice.

'For the life of a creature is in the blood, and I have given it to you to make atonement for yourselves on the altar.'
Leviticus 17:11a

RESPOND
'There is a fountain filled with blood, drawn from Immanuel's veins, and sinners plunged beneath that flood lose all their guilty stains' (William Cowper 1731–1800).

. . . .

Bible in a year: Judges 7,8; Mark 2

Friday 14 April
Leviticus 18:1–30

Distinctive lifestyle

PREPARE
'Do not conform to the pattern of this world, but be transformed by the renewing of your mind' (Romans 12:2). Ask God to shape your thinking.

READ
Leviticus 18:1–30

EXPLORE

Few Christians today would see the necessity of observing the rules about the consumption of blood in Leviticus 17. Are these rules about sexual relationships similarly outmoded? As the book of Hebrews makes clear (Hebrews 9,10), Jesus' sacrifice means that the blood of animal sacrifices is no longer needed, but there is nothing in the New Testament to suggest that these sexual standards have been superseded.

Having rescued them from Egypt (where all kinds of sexual relationships were practised), to take them to a land occupied by tribes whose worship of fertility gods included ritual prostitution and child sacrifice, the Lord calls his people to a distinctive lifestyle. The importance of family relationships and the protection of the vulnerable are still central in modern society today.

To what extent should Christians expect others to observe their values? In the latter half of the twentieth century, Mary Whitehouse, motivated by her Christian faith, became famous in the UK for her campaign against the 'permissive society'. Much derided in her lifetime, she has more recently been viewed as someone who warned of the impact on children of unregulated pornography before the dangers were widely recognised.

> 'You must not do as they do in Egypt, where you used to live, and you must not do as they do in the land of Canaan, where I am bringing you. Do not follow their practices.'

Leviticus 18:3

RESPOND
Pray for those suffering from the effects of harmful relationships, and those struggling to maintain a godly lifestyle.

Bible in a year: Judges 9,10; Mark 3

Practical holiness

PREPARE
As you approach this long passage ask the Lord to speak to you about the most important points for you today.

READ
Leviticus 19:1–37

EXPLORE
The first two verses make it clear that these instructions are for all the Israelites, because they are all God's holy people. The Ten Commandments are applied to their current situation, giving us principles to guide in applying them to our own lives.

Loving God not only entails a ban on worshipping idols or consulting the spirits of the dead. It also means that worship entails giving only the best to God (vs 5–8) and offering the first fruits to him (vs 23–25).

Many of the commands are about the right treatment of those less fortunate: the poor; the resident alien; the physically handicapped; slaves. The rule against stealing is applied to the subtle ways in which one can take advantage of others, for example by paying unjust wages. Generosity is encouraged; landowners are not to make the maximum profit from their land but should leave some for those who have little (see Ruth 2). It is no accident that churches have often been in the forefront of demands for social justice.

The guiding principle in these rules about dealings with other people is the phrase which Jesus said (alongside love for God) was one of the greatest commandments (Matthew 22:39), which Paul said summed up the commandments (Romans 13:9) and James called the royal law (James 2:8): 'Love your neighbour as yourself.'

'Do not seek revenge or bear a grudge against anyone among your people, but love your neighbour as yourself.'
Leviticus 19:18

RESPOND
Pray for victims of injustice in the news and those involved in working for justice.

Bible in a year: Judges 11,12; Psalms 42,43

Sunday 16 April
Psalm 89

Honest worship

PREPARE
Sing or listen to the hymn 'How Great Thou Art' or another praise song.

. . . .

READ
Psalm 89

EXPLORE
How many references to the Lord's love and faithfulness can you find in this psalm? Other versions use 'steadfast love' or 'unfailing love' to translate the Hebrew word rendered 'love' in the NIV. God deserves praise not only for his incomparable power in creation, but for his reliable love to his people.

In Leviticus we read of the God who has called his people and set them apart (eg Leviticus 20:26). Writing from a later standpoint the psalmist looks back on the way in which David was called and set apart to be king (v 20). The faithful God has made a covenant with David and his heirs, a promise to have a king over Israel for ever (v 29).

After praise to this loving, faithful, powerful covenant God we come to a problem. Disaster has come upon the people, the king is defeated and enemies rejoice (vs 38–45). We know that a much greater king than David has come and that his rule will last for ever, but the psalm comes from a time when the Lord seems to have turned his back on them (v 46).

When God seems far away, the best response may be to remember the love of the faithful Lord who redeemed us, tell him of the awfulness of the present situation and say, with the psalmist, 'Praise be to the LORD for ever' (v 52).

I will declare that your love stands firm for ever, that you have established your faithfulness in heaven itself.
Psalm 89:2

> ## RESPOND
> Pray for someone you know in distress, or for your own situation, as appropriate.

. . . .

Bible in a year: Judges 13,14; Mark 4

The wages of sin

PREPARE
Meditate on Colossians 3:5: 'Put to death, therefore, whatever belongs to your earthly nature.'

. . . .

READ
Leviticus 20:1–27

EXPLORE
Chapter 18 listed offences to be avoided by the Israelites; this chapter lists the punishments for such sins. Do they seem extreme? Those banned acts could have devastating effects in a community built around tight family units.

The emphasis on the importance of sexual purity and commitment to one God is in stark contrast to the people who lived in the land of Canaan. Sexual abandon and worship of idols went together; fertility rites and sacred prostitution were involved in the worship of Baal and other gods. Once in the Promised Land, the Israelites were repeatedly seduced into the worship of these foreign gods (eg 1 Kings 11:7).

When the people of Israel occupy the Promised Land, God will tell them to take drastic action to remove all traces of idolatry. God's people are to avoid the religious and sexual licence which was rife among the surrounding tribes. God has set them apart to be his people (vs 24,26). The Ten Commandments were not given to enable people to earn God's favour; they were given to people whom God had already made his own (Exodus 20:2).

As Christians our motivation to live holy lives is to please the one who has made us his own (Ephesians 4:20–24). Where do you find this challenging?

'You are to be holy to me because I, the LORD, am holy, and I have set you apart from the nations to be my own.'
Leviticus 20:26

RESPOND
Pray for Christians in parliament and those who advise them as they seek to balance personal freedom with moral standards in legislation.

. . . .

Bible in a year: Judges 15,16; Mark 5

Tuesday 18 April
Leviticus 21:1–24

Exemplary leaders

PREPARE
Give thanks for Jesus, the High Priest who intercedes for us.

....

READ
Leviticus 21:1–24

EXPLORE
I read an article in today's newspaper about the problems of a large church in trouble because of its leader's relationship problems. By the time you read these notes there will doubtless be another similar story in the news; the world expects high standards from religious leaders. In this chapter it seems that God also expects a higher standard of holiness from his priests.

Leviticus was given to a people for whom priests have a unique role. How should we apply it today? We have a sinless High Priest, who offered a perfect sacrifice, in the Most Holy Place (Hebrews 9:11,12). Christians are 'a royal priesthood, a holy nation' (1 Peter 2:9), so we all have an obligation to holiness. Is it reasonable to expect Christian leaders (and their families) to set an example in their lifestyle?

Do the restrictions in verses 16 to 23 seem discriminatory to our ears?

Imagine the newspaper headlines if Christian denominations refused to ordain someone who was handicapped. The Old Testament priests had a unique role in representing the people to God, but also of being God's representatives. In the Holy Place only the perfect was allowed. Levites whose physical handicap prevented them offering sacrifices were, however, permitted to share in the sacrificed food, along with the other Levites.

> Priests must be holy. They must be set apart for me. I am their God.
>
> **Leviticus 21:6a (NIRV)**

RESPOND
Pray for the leaders of your church to stay close to the Lord, and for those who have been harmed by the actions of church leaders.

....

Bible in a year: Judges 17,18; Mark 6

Only the best

PREPARE
'Cleanse me from my sin, Lord, put thy power within, Lord. Take me as I am, Lord, and make me all thine own'.*

. . . .

READ
Leviticus 22:1–33

EXPLORE
The Covid-19 pandemic made us all aware of the need to avoid infection and, if one became infected, the importance of not passing it on. Uncleanliness in Old Testament times was seen as contagious. It was impossible to avoid totally, but it had to be dealt with before a priest could touch anything that was to be offered to God. Only the best could be offered, and only by ceremonially clean people.

Leviticus chapters 11 to 15 deal with clean and unclean things. Certain animals were unclean and could not be offered to God. There were also many things that could render a person unclean, such as touching a corpse or certain diseases (vs 4,5). Rituals could be followed to make a person clean again (vs 4–8). Today, most liturgies and patterns for personal prayer include confession near the beginning; as we approach the Lord, we first ask for his cleansing from sin.

In Old Testament times, only the best could be brought to this holy Lord in sacrifice. With finite resources it must have been tempting for a farmer to give to God an animal that was lame, or one which could not be used for breeding. Faith was needed to sacrifice the best to God.

'... if any of your descendants is ceremonially unclean and yet comes near the sacred offerings that the Israelites consecrate to the Lord, that person must be cut off from my presence. I am the Lord.'
Leviticus 22:3

RESPOND
Are there any ways in which you give God less than the best? How could you change this?

*R Hudson Pope, 1879–1967, © SGM International

. . . .

Bible in a year: Judges 19,20; Psalm 44

Thursday 20 April
Leviticus 23:1–22

Celebrating God's goodness

PREPARE
How do you celebrate your favourite time of the Christian year?

READ
Leviticus 23:1–22

EXPLORE
After a reminder of the importance of the sabbath rest principle (v 3), the people of Israel are given an annual calendar of feast days on which the whole nation should gather before God. Today we look at the ones that fall in spring (in the northern hemisphere); tomorrow's reading looks at the autumn festivals. For the spring feasts there are clear parallels in the New Testament.

The first to be celebrated are Passover and the associated Feast of Unleavened Bread, reminders of their miraculous escape from Egypt (vs 4–8). For Paul, Christ is the Passover Lamb, for whom we should remove the leaven of evil from our lives (1 Corinthians 5:7,8).

The Feast of Firstfruits (vs 9–14) marked a time when harvest was begun with an offering to the Lord, before any produce was used for human consumption (v 14). Paul sees Christ's resurrection as the first fruit of the resurrection of the dead (1 Corinthians 15:23).

Fifty days later the Feast of Weeks marks the completion of the harvest and celebrates the Lord's provision (v 16). With this, there is a reminder to leave the edges of fields (v 22); thanksgiving goes hand in hand with concern for the poor. This feast became known as Pentecost, and it was on this feast that the Holy Spirit was given to the first believers (Acts 2:1–4).

'These are the LORD's appointed festivals, the sacred assemblies you are to proclaim at their appointed times.'
Leviticus 23:4

RESPOND
Meditate on one of the feast days. Imagine being a participant in the celebration, then rejoice in its fulfilment in Christ.

Bible in a year: Judges 21; Mark 7

Happy New Year!

PREPARE
Give thanks for material blessings.

....

READ
Leviticus 23:23–44

EXPLORE
For an agricultural community, the cycle of the seasons is important; for the Israelites, the end of the old year and the beginning of the new is marked with the sounding of trumpets (not brass but rams' horns) (v 24). Nowadays Jews around the world mark this feast as Rosh Hashanah. It ushers in the holiest month.

The Day of Atonement (vs 26,27) has been described in detail in chapter 16. For many people today, New Year is a time to reflect on the past year and make resolutions for the coming 12 months (which rarely last more than a couple of weeks!). This Day of Atonement offered a way to be rid of the sins of the past. It anticipated the perfect 'once for all' sacrifice that Jesus would make for the sins of the world (Hebrews 7:27).

The Festival of Booths (or Tabernacles) would remind the Israelites, after they had settled in the Promised Land, of their journey through the wilderness. By living for a week each year in a temporary shelter they would not forget the journey that God had brought them on (vs 42,43). Yesterday I happened to visit the area where I lived while doing my first job. It made me think about the course my life has taken since then. Sometimes it is good to look back and reflect on God's leading through life.

'These are the LORD's appointed festivals, which you are to proclaim as sacred assemblies for bringing food offerings to the LORD.'
Leviticus 23:37a

RESPOND
Reflect on the times when you have known God's leading or provision and bring your current situation to him.

Bible in a year: Ruth 1,2; Mark 8

Saturday 22 April
Leviticus 24:1–23

Give me oil in my lamp

PREPARE
Thank God that we can enter his presence freely.

....

READ
Leviticus 24:1–23

EXPLORE
After details of the annual festivals come instructions for the ongoing maintenance of the Holy Place. It is a reminder that the maintenance of regular worship is as important as the great celebrations. While the Most Holy Place – containing the Ark of the Covenant – was visited by the High Priest only once a year, priests entered the Holy Place to burn incense each morning and evening (v 7).

The Holy Place also contained a gold-covered table and a golden lampstand on which were seven lamps (see Exodus 25:23–40). Olive oil was used to fuel the lamps (which provided the only light in the Holy Place) and the lamps burned continually (v 2). On the table were 12 loaves of bread, representing the 12 tribes of Israel; these were replaced weekly (vs 5,8). The life of faith cannot be sustained only by occasional celebrations but by regular refreshment.

Guidance is sought from the Lord about a particular case of blasphemy; the commandment (Exodus 20:7) did not prescribe a punishment. Today, we live in different times. Is there a danger of us becoming inured to the casual misuse of the Lord's name?

If 'an eye for an eye' seems harsh, we must remember that it gives a limit to punishment. And notice that crimes against property were not punished as harshly as crimes against other people (v 21). Jesus goes further: turn the other cheek (Matthew 5:39).

'The lamps on the pure gold lampstand before the Lord must be tended continually.'
Leviticus 24:4

RESPOND
Pray for Christians accused of blasphemy in Islamic societies.

....

Bible in a year: Ruth 3,4; Psalm 45

Our eternal home

PREPARE
Where do you feel at home?

....

READ
Psalm 90

EXPLORE
The psalm's heading, 'A prayer of Moses', might lead you to imagine the aged Moses, after his long journey through the wilderness, standing at the edge of the Promised Land (but unable to enter it), reflecting on life's highs and lows (Deuteronomy 4:21–24).

The psalm begins with a reminder of the eternal God's faithfulness to his people. We have read in Leviticus of God's dwelling place among his people as they travel to a new home in the Promised Land. Here, the psalmist sees the Lord himself as the permanent home in which his people live (v 1). Home is defined not by location but by relationship.

The psalmist prays for a heart of wisdom which comes from seeing the fleeting nature of our lives in the light of God's eternal plan (v 12). Though all may crumble around us, and we are aware of the impermanence of life, it is good to be reminded that God's love is unfailing (v 14). It's no surprise that Isaac Watts' paraphrase of this psalm, 'O God our help in ages past', is a favourite at funerals and is sung at London's annual remembrance service.

Avoiding the extremes of panic in the face of uncertainty or complacency, in the security of being at home in God, the psalmist prays for God to be at work through all he does (v 17).

Teach us to number our days, that we may gain a heart of wisdom.

Psalm 90:12

RESPOND
O God, our help in ages past, /
Our hope for years to come, / Still
be our guard while troubles last, /
And our eternal home!
(Isaac Watts, 1719)*

---

*For other verses see https://hymnary.org/hymn/CYBER/4892

....

Bible in a year: 1 Samuel 1–3; Mark 9

Monday 24 April
Leviticus 25:1–55

Jubilee year

PREPARE
'Open my eyes that I may see wonderful things in your law' (Psalm 119:18).

. . . .

READ
Leviticus 25:1–55

EXPLORE
These instructions, for the Israelites to follow when settled in the Promised Land, might sound revolutionary to our twenty-first-century western ears. But they address problems we face today too.

This sabbath principle applies to farming (vs 1–7). Every seventh year the land is to be rested and left fallow. We know that not overworking the soil is good sense, but it required faith to believe that God's provision in the sixth year would last. Our minds can so easily be trapped into thinking that fulfilment and security can only be found in acquiring material wealth.

Even more faith is required when a further rest year is announced – the Jubilee year (vs 8–12). This is a reminder to landowners that they only hold in trust what is God's: land was to be returned to the families who owned it when the Promised Land was first occupied (v 23). In effect, land was leased at a price until the next Jubilee. Anyone who had lost his home through debt had to be given the chance to redeem it; failing that, a member of the family should be given the opportunity (eg vs 25–55; see also Ruth 2:20). If all else failed, an impoverished Israelite might become a slave of a fellow Israelite – but only until the Jubilee.

'Consecrate the fiftieth year and proclaim liberty throughout the land to all its inhabitants. It shall be a jubilee for you.'
Leviticus 25:10a

RESPOND
Pray for a Christian organisation responding to environmental crises, poverty, personal debt or global debt.

. . . .

Bible in a year: 1 Samuel 4–6; Mark 10

Covenant God

PREPARE
'Give thanks to the LORD, for he is good; his love endures for ever' (Psalm 118:1).

. . . .

READ
Leviticus 26:1–46

EXPLORE
It was common for ancient legal agreements to end with a section of blessings and curses, but this is different. After a reminder of the things which make them unique – a lack of idols, observance of sabbaths and God's presence in the sanctuary – God promises that if they obey, they will see prosperity and peace in the Promised Land. More than that, the Lord himself will walk among them (v 12).

Or, if they fail to listen to the Lord and obey his commands, they will face judgement. There are escalating stages of punishment: a simple reversal of the blessing, through crop failure, wild beasts and foreign invasion, to removal from the land into exile. Each punishment section is prefaced by an 'if you will not listen to me' (vs 14,18,21,23,27). These sanctions are intended to turn the wayward people back to the Lord.

Yet, even if all the warnings are ignored and the people are exiled, God would still be ready and waiting for them to repent so that they may return to the Promised Land and enjoy the blessings of the covenant God made with Abraham (vs 40–45).

The people would repeatedly stray from the Lord. But eventually, on return from exile, repentance brings reconciliation, the Temple of the Lord is rebuilt and worship re-established (read more in Ezra and Nehemiah).

'I will walk among you and be your God, and you will be my people.'
Leviticus 26:12

RESPOND
Are there areas in your life where you need to return to the Lord's ways?

. . . .

Bible in a year: 1 Samuel 7–9; Mark 11

Wednesday 26 April
Leviticus 27:1–34

Fulfilling vows

PREPARE
What does it mean to offer yourself as a living sacrifice (see Romans 12:1)?

··

READ
Leviticus 27:1–34

EXPLORE
I have met people who, facing life-threatening situations, have prayed, 'God, if you get me out of this, I will always serve you' (or something similar). Others, after a particular blessing from God, may promise to give something to him. This passage works out the details for times when an Israelite vowed to dedicate someone or something to God.

If the giver, or a member of their household, is dedicated to the Lord, they would be unable to serve as a priest, as only a member of the tribe of Levi can serve in this way. They could work in support of the Levites, or a gift of money be substituted. The prices given reflect the amount of work a person could perform in a labour-intensive economy. The instructions are also about the value of other gifts, such as animals and property. If the donor wishes to buy them back, a premium is added.

There are warnings too. When God demands unholy things to be destroyed (eg Deuteronomy 2:34,35), they cannot be redeemed. When tithes are due, the giver must not try to cheat God (vs 30–33).

People will always find ways to avoid their obligations to God. Jesus criticised some religious people for using the excuse that resources were dedicated to God (*Corban*), to avoid the obligation to look after their parents (Mark 7:9–13).

> 'A tithe of everything from the land, whether grain from the soil or fruit from the trees, belongs to the LORD; it is holy to the LORD.'
> **Leviticus 27:30**

RESPOND
What has struck you most in these chapters of Leviticus? Pray for help to live as one of God's holy people.

··

Bible in a year: 1 Samuel 10,11; Psalms 46,47

The way of truth

Letters are meant to be read from start to finish in one sitting; this one is the same, written to a trusted friend, 'my true son in ... faith' and a co-worker, by Paul.

In the face of increasing threat by false teachers who were determined to distort the Christian message, Paul writes to Titus (in Crete) in great detail to instruct and authorise the teaching of 'sound doctrine' (1:9) where this new faith had only just started to take shape. The very existence of this new group of people called Christians was being threatened, in particular by the 'circumcision party' (1:10). Not only did they demand adherence to the Mosaic regulations but also denied Christ's resurrection, incarnation and death: fundamentals of the Christian faith. In the midst of this inhospitable environment, with the young church struggling, this communication arrives as encouragement and instruction for the leaders.

The letter begins with a discussion about truth and falsehood. It then moves to teaching about the conduct of believers (1:2,3) and concludes with a heartfelt statement of what God has done in Christ and what that means for those who sign up to this (3:3–8)!

If there is one thing that is imperative before you get into the series, it is the reading of the whole letter in one go – do it! It took me exactly 6 minutes and 10 seconds. Hold the Bible and stand up to read it out loud; feel the urgency of what these Cretan Christians are being called to live out because of God's saving work for all.

About the writer
Nudrat Malik

A Pakistani, Christian immigrant, Nudrat has only recently started describing herself as Asian British, despite having lived in England for most of her adult life. She lives with her family in Buckinghamshire, where she enjoys a recently discovered love of gardening.

Thursday 27 April

Titus 1:1–9

Nature of truth

PREPARE:
'As the Sun of Righteousness dawns in our hearts anoint our lips with the seal of your Spirit that we may witness to your gospel and sing your praise in all the earth'.*

READ

Titus 1:1–9

EXPLORE

Does truth need a guardian or an ambassador? If the well-known saying is to be believed, the truth 'will out' no matter what! But what we see in the world around us gives us little hope that this will really happen.

For Paul, an essential part of the growing church must be leaders who know, understand, teach and live 'sound doctrine' – the truth (v 9). And to this end, the role of an overseer is paramount: encourage the truth and refute that which is not. Those with leadership responsibility will have to find many and varied ways of doing both. Consider for a moment which aspect of the given two you would find challenging.

Though daunting, the list of behaviours given here is the hallmark of a person who has experienced (and continues to experience) the transformational work of the Holy Spirit in their life, encompassing the whole of life: family relationships, habits, personality (vs 4–9). This is a transformation that requires our collaboration: discipline, resilience and stamina. The elder must be someone who understands and exhibits these qualities in the face of the fight between falsehood and truth – a fight that still rages on today (v 9).

> Paul, a servant of God and an apostle of Jesus Christ to further the faith of God's elect and their knowledge of the truth that leads to godliness...
>
> **Titus 1:1**

RESPOND
Pray for groups that are involved in representing or fighting for truth.

Common Worship Morning Prayer: Epiphany Season

Bible in a year: 1 Samuel 12,13; Mark 12

Fruit of truth

PREPARE
Repeat these words: 'I will give thanks to you, LORD, with all my heart; I will tell of all your wonderful deeds. I will be glad and rejoice in you; I will sing the praises of your name, O Most High' (see Psalm 9:1,2).

READ
Titus 1:10–16

EXPLORE
This new community of Christians appears to have more than its fair share of challenges: false teaching, determined deceivers, people who are in it only for themselves and those who are plain and simple hypocrites (vs 10–12)! I'm reminded of Christ's teaching about the fruit which a tree bears: it is the clearest witness to the health of the tree (Matthew 7:16).

Paul's urgent and stark words express the necessity for the building up of this group of Christians who are, spiritually speaking, in their infancy. Without this, they will be unable to produce fruit, which must be their primary focus. They have received 'knowledge of the truth' (Titus 1:1), which speaks of the true God; therefore their lives must be witnesses to this. Truthfulness and purity should stand out in their lives, because without these, this community will be in jeopardy (v 15) – just the same as salt losing its saltiness (Matthew 5:13).

How apt these words are for the twenty-first-century Christian who inhabits a postmodern world of fast fashion, pursuit of perfection, intolerance and dissatisfaction with ourselves.

> They claim to know God, but by their actions they deny him. They are detestable, disobedient and unfit for doing anything good.

Titus 1:16

RESPOND
Look at the news headlines. 'Sort' news items into the following categories: truth and falsehood. What are the consequences for people involved? How far-reaching are the implications? Individual, family or ethnic group? Pray that truth will be heard.

Bible in a year: 1 Samuel 14,15; Mark 13

Saturday 29 April

Titus 2:1–10

Living with imperfection

PREPARE

Listen to the song 'Father, Let your Kingdom Come' by Porter's Gate* or simply meditate on 'Alleluia – Father, let your kingdom come'.

....

READ

Titus 2:1–10

EXPLORE

This new group of Christians in Crete inhabited a world less than favourable for growth in their faith. Recognising the limitations of a given situation may make us behave in ways that are less than our preferred set of actions. We say things like, 'Well, this is the best we can do under the given circumstances.' Despite this human tendency, Paul's words list uncompromising requirements in the behaviour of these believers.

His words suggest that such reasoning is not a valid way of thinking for those who have realised what the saving work is that God has done for them. Actions must point to that grace and love of God at work in their lives. We, like all other believers, become partners with God in his work on earth because we have experienced the overflowing love of God towards us (vs 4–7). Our attitude and example-setting behaviour towards those closest to us must witness to this reality.

Is Paul asking for perfection? Surely that's not real life! But the reality is that it is only in community that we find ourselves truly. Community makes or breaks us! All the more reason that this *distinct* community of people, with a particular identity and flavour, should exhibit qualities of respect, self-control, integrity and soundness in faith and love.

> In everything set them an example by doing what is good ... so that those who oppose you may ... have nothing bad to say about us.

Titus 2:7,8

RESPOND

Spend time in quiet before God. Make your family relationships a focus for today's prayers and allow the Holy Spirit to continue his work of transformation in your life.

*www.youtube.comwatch?v=EHIGm7qYVz4

....

Bible in a year: 1 Samuel 16,17; Psalm 48

In his shadow

PREPARE
Read today's psalm two or three times, if possible using different translations.

....

READ
Psalm 91

EXPLORE
When everything around seems uncertain and unpredictable, it is only natural to search for something that will give certainty and security. That is what a good friend of mine decided to do. His search for a rock-solid guarantee of something or someone who would take care of him as he faced many challenges came after a long period of ignoring God. It was only after he had exhausted all other possible avenues of help and support that he 'gave in' to God. Self-assurance, pride, stubbornness and a genuine belief that asking God for help really was off the beaten track had kept him from finding refuge in the Almighty.

This psalm reminds the believer that the Most High is the source of refuge in the midst of trouble (v 2). It also asks readers to nurture trust in God, entrusting one's whole life to him. Let's not overlook the profound truth that this transcendent God, the Most High, seeks to enter into relationship with those who engage with him (verse 9: 'If you say...'). The psalmist invites us to try out this 'dwelling place' because it offers protection from everything that may threaten you – all you have to do is take a chance on God's care and love for you, which does not have a 'use by' date (vs 14–16).

> 'Because he loves me,' says the LORD, 'I will rescue him; I will protect him, for he acknowledges my name.'
> **Psalm 91:14**

RESPOND
Here are two distinct images of God's protection: a fortress and the wings of a bird. Given the challenges of life for you at this moment, which would you prefer? Rest in his care now.

....

Bible in a year: 1 Samuel 18,19; Mark 14

Monday 1 May

Titus 2:11–15

New humanity 1

PREPARE

'Give thanks to the Lord, for he is good. His love endures for ever' (Psalm 136:1).

....

READ

Titus 2:11–15

EXPLORE

Future anticipation of something always makes us behave differently in the here and now. For example, booking a holiday means we buy sun lotion or a few items of clothing that will suit the weather. Or think of Marty, the main character in the movie *Back to the Future*, who pursues a particular course of action because he knows what the future will be like.

The confidence that must fill the Cretan Christians is based on so much more: the saving work of Christ has already been done and it can be realised in the present (vs 11,12)! His work of non-judgemental, generous acceptance which extends to all, not just a few, must make the present different. This means change – not accepting the world as it is, but working towards a world as it should be. A world that is marked with kindness and justice, God-willed not self-willed, and doing

'what is good' (v 14). Because Christians have experienced the powerful love and grace of God, it must inform the way they live as they wait for Jesus' return (v 13). Paul reminds people that they must have confidence in 'the grace of God' so that their lives become evidence that the future is already here!

> For the grace of God has appeared that offers salvation to all people.
>
> **Titus 2:11**

RESPOND

Make a concerted effort to look out for actions that speak of God's saving work in a person's life. Be willing and prepared to be surprised where you might see this. Have eyes that see and ears that hear (Matthew 13:16).

....

Bible in a year: 1 Samuel 20–22; Mark 15

Tuesday 2 May
Titus 3:1–15

New humanity 2

PREPARE
Listen to some contemplative music of your choice as you prepare to read God's Word and pray.

. . . .

READ
Titus 3:1–15

EXPLORE
As his letter draws to a close, Paul once again takes the opportunity to spell out the essentials of the Christian faith – as if reciting a familiar liturgy that does not change. You can almost imagine Paul, like a teacher, writing an equation on the whiteboard, explaining how one part of it must result in the other: because of the Holy Spirit, you are a new human (vs 4–7)!

The shape, size and appearance of renewed humanity may not look very much different from the old, but what comes forth is remarkable. It is as if to define a human being would be to list the following characteristics: good towards others, peaceable, humble, kind, loving, free and not a slave to any self-satisfying desires. Then, just in case there is any chance of misunderstanding, Paul clarifies that the Holy Spirit poured generously into their lives is what makes the equation work (vs 5,6)!

There is one other aspect to this new humanity that makes this new creation so very different: they are to make others the focus. Paul urges believers to devote themselves to generous, helpful actions on behalf of the wider community (vs 13,14). This is the way of truth (v 8).

> ... he saved us, not because of righteous things we had done, but because of his mercy ... through the washing of rebirth and renewal by the Holy Spirit...

Titus 3:5

RESPOND
What acts of service for the community are you involved in? Are there other aspects of being a renewed human being that you find challenging? Bring your thoughts and ideas prayerfully before God.

. . . .

Bible in a year: 1 Samuel 23,24; Mark 16

WAY IN
Obadiah and Nahum

God takes no prisoners

About the writer
Liz Pacey

Liz runs her local charity Knitwits group. She enjoys regular speaking engagements, talking about knitting, books, disgraceful old age. Or anything really...

'To take no prisoners' means to be ruthlessly aggressive or uncompromising in the pursuit of one's objectives. And this is absolutely the God we are presented with in the books of Obadiah and Nahum. He is not for turning. No one is invincible when God is around.

Nahum tells of the forthcoming judgement on the cruel Assyrians who live in Nineveh. Obadiah speaks about the ancient feud between Edom and Israel, which will conclude with the exiles repatriated. In both cases blood will be spilt. Justice, pride and judgement are important themes. Justice must prevail, whatever the cost to the perpetrators of the evil. And better things are in store for those who have suffered at the hands of the proud.

Here we have two so-called 'minor' prophets, both speaking out bravely with stirring and powerful messages that would certainly not please the oppressors. Nahum and Obadiah are both very much in touch with the harsh realities of the world they live in – very good reason for them to be called to share God's Word in difficult times. We too need to be on the ball to be effective as God's spokespeople. As we hear news reports and see war-torn disaster areas on our television screens, we can begin to imagine what it was like for the people of Nineveh and Edom. We can be thankful that our God has a great track record for bringing good out of evil.

Pride goes before a fall

PREPARE
Have you ever been proud – in an arrogant way – of something you've achieved? Were you brought back to earth with a bump? How did you feel then? Ask God to keep you honest and humble in his sight today.

....

READ
Obadiah

EXPLORE
The Edomites were literally able to look down on other people. They had a sense of superiority, not particularly because of what they'd done, but because of where they lived, high up in the mountains (v 3). This influenced their whole outlook on life. They came to feel unassailable, feeling no sympathy for the misfortunes of others (v 12). Do we ever get so locked into our own concerns that we forget about other people and their needs? Does our status in life ever cause us to be proud and perhaps prone to look down on others?

Obadiah warns that the day of the Lord is near, and things are about to change for these proud mountaintop dwellers (v 15). Verse 17 sings out to us: for God's people on Mount Zion there will be deliverance. It will be a holy place. In the midst of devastation (v 13), the returning exiles will have their starting point to recreate all that is good and godly (v 20). Jacob (God's people) will possess his inheritance (v 17), '… And the kingdom will be the Lord's' (v 21). God is in control.

> But on Mount Zion will be deliverance; it will be holy, and Jacob will possess his inheritance.
>
> **Obadiah 17**

RESPOND
Thank God that, whatever trials our world is currently facing, he knows and is in control.

....

Bible in a year: 1 Samuel 25,26; Psalm 49

God is our refuge

PREPARE
Imagine your life as a rollercoaster. Do you feel God with you in the most frightening parts of the ride? Thank him for bringing you safely through turmoil and challenges.

....

READ
Nahum 1

EXPLORE
I've never been on a rollercoaster, but this passage resonates with images I've seen of them. They are scary! There is rapid acceleration through the first six verses as God's anger builds up through natural forces. The earth itself trembles (v 5). Then there is a little – but significant – pause in verse 7. An oasis in the storm. God cares for all who trust in him. Then momentum picks up again. God really is on the warpath against the warmongering, idolatrous Nineveh (of Jonah fame more than a century earlier) – and heaven help his foes (v 8)! Another pause in verse 15: peace at last.

How would we survive in life without the pauses, the times when we can be sheltered from the forces and storms around us? Would we cope without God's care? Sometimes, it's hard to accept our peace when we know others elsewhere are suffering.

In our rollercoaster lives we can be flung battered onto the pause. Sometimes we have to make a determined effort to breathe and take in a little piece of God's goodness before we are off again.

> The LORD is good, a refuge in times of trouble. He cares for those who trust in him...
>
> **Nahum 1:7**

RESPOND
Take time out today to pause and pray for someone you know who needs the promise of calm and security in their lives. Ask God to show you how you might be a place of refuge for them.

....

Bible in a year: 1 Samuel 27,28; 1 Corinthians 1

Conquering heroes

PREPARE
Imagine the relief Judah (1:15) must have felt when its people realised their enemy was going to be defeated. Ask God to burst through the walls that imprison you.

READ
Nahum 2

EXPLORE
Nahum warns that attack is coming and the people of Nineveh need to act. But now God will be the lion hunter (vs 11–13). His words are short and sharp (v 1). In times of distress there is no place for long words.

Attacks on people can take many forms. My husband has Alzheimer's. Sometimes it's hard to see God in this. We – Norman particularly – are living in a kind of exile. A lot of life that we took for granted has been, pretty much without warning, swallowed up in our new roles of cared for and carer. But with a lot of support, professional and personal, we brace ourselves and marshal all our strength (v 1).

So many of us live with things in our lives beyond our control. We all have to do whatever we can, with whatever we have, whatever our circumstances. God may seem distant sometimes but we know he is there – he is in control – and has the power to restore us (v 2). Nineveh, Judah's enemy, would be destroyed.

> The LORD will restore the splendour of Jacob like the splendour of Israel, though destroyers have laid them waste and have ruined their vines.

Nahum 2:2

RESPOND
'Thank you, Lord, for the land you have given me to inhabit. It may not seem like a land of milk and honey, but it is the furrow you have called me to plough. You are with me through thick and thin. Amen.'

Bible in a year: 1 Samuel 29–31; 1 Corinthians 2

Fight, not flight

PREPARE

Do you ever want to fly away from your troubles? Praise God that however disastrous our outer circumstances may appear, inside we can be rooted in him: 'For in him we live and move and have our being' (Acts 17:28).

READ
Nahum 3

EXPLORE

The grassy slope was wet and muddy. Being a sturdy lass, I took control of the dog to negotiate the descent. There was no way I would be pulled over. Well… you can guess the rest! Thankfully, only my pride was hurt.

It is so easy to slide down a slippery slope! And once started, it's hard to stop. It's virtually impossible not to involve other people in the descent too. In this passage we see the far-reaching effects of the descent away from God that Nineveh experienced under the powerful, false-god-worshipping Assyrians. They'd had a giddy rise to prosperity, but now the merchants have upped and gone, taking their assets with them (vs 16,17). They aren't going to hang around when it has all gone pear-shaped. Lethargy descends on the city (v 18).

Sometimes it might be the right thing to make a new start, but we have to be very careful that we are not running away from our problems. Are you a fighter? Do you get tough with your problems, or just inelegantly slide into the mud?

You have increased the number of your merchants till they are more numerous than the stars in the sky, but like locusts they strip the land and then fly away.

Nahum 3:16

RESPOND

'Lord God, may I begin each new day in hope and thanksgiving, and end it with a sense of your overcoming love and power in my life. May I never shirk what you would have me do. Amen.'

Bible in a year: 2 Samuel 1,2; Psalm 50

With a flourish

PREPARE

How beautiful are trees: their stretching out heavenwards; the shelter they give; the statement they make. What kind of tree might you see yourself as? Praise God for his creation and thank him that you are part of it.

....

READ
Psalm 92

EXPLORE

I feel as though, in our readings this week through Obadiah and Nahum, we have held our breath as disaster followed disaster and God's anger was heaped down on his enemies. But today there is a gear change in this Sabbath psalm. There is still talk of evildoers and destruction (v 7), but mainly we are concerned with a man addressing God directly and very personally. He trusts God in a way the people of Nineveh and Edom did not (v 6). He can look forward. They could only look back.

I love the word 'flourish' (v 12). Here, it sends such a powerfully positive message. It makes me think of a dramatic gesture. The tree not only grows (v 12), but grows with style and panache. Evildoers may flourish, but are short-lived, like grass (v 7). It is easy to mow down grass. But a tree? A tree planted in the house of God will flourish, even when it grows old (v 14). And, for those of us who have already reached a certain maturity of age, that is welcome news! Praise God!

> The righteous will flourish like a palm tree, they will grow like a cedar of Lebanon; planted in the house of the LORD, they will flourish...
>
> **Psalm 92:12,13**

RESPOND

Get a sheet of paper and sign your name – with a flourish! Thank God for your life in him and ask him to help you to be his signature in our world.

....

Bible in a year: 2 Samuel 3–5; 1 Corinthians 3

IT'S YOUR MOVE

YOUR SECONDARY SCHOOL SURVIVAL GUIDE

- Over 2 million children helped to settle into a new school through this series.

- A great way to support children in your local schools.

- Includes a survival guide, survival journal and survival stories to help children adapt to a new school.

- Additional content available online.

Different times, same God

Whichever part of the world you live in, life in the twenty-first century must seem a long way removed from life in the Middle East 3,000 years ago. But although cultures and accepted practices change, people are still people, with the same range of emotions, the same aspirations to live well and to honour God, but also with the same tendencies to fail and value ourselves more highly than we ought! Fortunately, though, God is still the same God, whose nature is to love fallen humans, to be generous, to show mercy, to offer fresh starts, but also to require wholehearted worship and allegiance. Looking at the life of King Solomon, we find much to warn, challenge, inspire and encourage us as we seek to follow God today.

For me, Solomon's story raises a number of questions:

- How does God work out his purposes through the scheming and machinations of self-serving ambitious people?

- Does God only accept worship from people who are wholehearted?

- Does God prefer some people to others?

- How do I make godly choices when faced with several bad options and no obviously good one?

- What is true wisdom?

I have written the 'Explore' sections of these notes as a diary of a fictional courtier in King Solomon's court (but look carefully at the Bible passages to check out his accounts!). As he observes, questions and comments on what he sees happening in Solomon's life, he tries to discern God's hand at work – and challenges us to do the same in our families, churches, communities and societies.

About the writer
Esther Bailey

Esther lives with her husband John in north-east England, close to the Angel of the North. She is working with URC churches in Gateshead, Chester-le-Street and Stanley to engage with children and families not previously part of the church. Esther and John love exploring new areas in their aged campervan.

Monday 8 May
1 Kings 1:1–27

Political intrigue

PREPARE
In controversial situations, how do you discern what is the right action to take? Can God work through human plotting and intrigue?

READ
1 Kings 1:1–27

EXPLORE
'First day in my new job and what a shock I got! I was expecting power and glory – King David has expanded our country so much, made us a force to be reckoned with, and utterly destroyed our old enemies, the Philistines. But instead, I have found an old man, losing his grip and not having the foresight to name his chosen successor... and much plotting and whispering in corners. I am going to have to be wise about the friendships I make if I want to keep my job!

'The obvious choice for successor is David's eldest surviving son, Adonijah, but there are those who say that Solomon is the one who is loved by the Lord God.

'With David oblivious to what is happening, Adonijah has declared himself king. He certainly looks regal enough and several of David's officials are endorsing his claim, but Nathan and Bathsheba seem to be planning a counterattack.

'I noticed that Adonijah, the son of Haggith (his name means "festive"), started his attempt at kingship with a party, whereas Bathsheba (whose name means "daughter of oath") appealed to an oath that David had supposedly made regarding Solomon.'

> 'My lord the king, the eyes of all Israel are on you, to learn from you who will sit on the throne of my lord the king after him.'
> **1 Kings 1:20**

RESPOND
Pray about any power struggles you are aware of, whether in your local church, in business, in politics or on the international stage. Ask God to direct things so that his purposes are worked out.

Bible in a year: 2 Samuel 6,7; 1 Corinthians 4

Counter moves

PREPARE
Jesus said: 'Blessed are the peacemakers' (Matthew 5:9). Sometimes making peace means actively confronting injustice or wrong. Can you think of examples of people who have done that?

....

READ
1 Kings 1:28–53

EXPLORE
'Well, it seems the old king still has it in him! He shouts out a few orders and people leap into action to do his bidding.

'Adonijah had had his coronation ceremony at the Stone of Zoheleth – a sacred spring (but rather out of the public eye). He was obviously not totally confident that David would endorse his kingship, so was trying to get it all done and present the nation with a fait accompli that could not be undone.

'But David showed emphatically that Solomon was his choice. He was mounted on David's own mule, taken to Gihon, the foremost sacred spring for his coronation, and brought back to take his seat on David's own throne. Moreover, this was done with much public display: trumpets blowing and crowds of people shouting and celebrating, "Long live King Solomon!"

'Through all the chaos of the day, two things struck me particularly. First, Benaiah's prayer that the Lord would make Solomon even greater than his father David – David was such a great king himself, I can't wait to see how God might answer that prayer! And secondly, Solomon's gracious response to Adonijah. As his name means, he is a man of peace!'

'Praise be to the LORD … who has allowed my eyes to see a successor on my throne today.'
1 Kings 1:48

RESPOND
Have you ever had to forgive someone who has wronged you, or work to put right a wrong situation? How has God's grace enabled you in those situations?

....

Bible in a year: 2 Samuel 8–10; 1 Corinthians 5

Wednesday 10 May
1 Kings 2:1–25

Unfinished business

PREPARE
Different leaders bring different skills to their roles. David was obviously not good at dealing with challenges to his authority, so he asks Solomon to deal with unfinished business. How willing are you to receive from others where your gifts are lacking?

READ
1 Kings 2:1–25

EXPLORE
'Since appointing Solomon his successor, David seems to have regained some energy and has been dealing with some matters of state that had been neglected recently. As I entered David's chamber this afternoon, I realised Solomon was with him, and they were discussing priorities for Solomon once David passes away. I was about to withdraw quietly when I heard them mention Joab.

'I was quite young at the time of Absalom's rebellion, but I remember the outrage that Joab might have ignored David's order not to harm Absalom and yet still retain his job as commander of the army. Maybe family pressure meant that David could not sack his nephew. A few years later, David did try to promote another one of his nephews over Joab. However, Joab apparently murdered him and still managed to keep his role. I noted that Joab had sided with Adonijah.

Was he just a career man with no morals? Was he loyal to no one but himself?

'What a contrast with David's advice to Solomon to observe what God requires and to walk in obedience with him.'

> '... observe what the LORD your God requires: walk in obedience to him, and keep his decrees and commands, his laws and regulations ... Do this so that you may prosper in all you do and wherever you go...'
> **1 Kings 2:3**

RESPOND
What leadership roles do you have? What are your strengths and weaknesses? Ask the Lord to equip you for the roles he has given you.

Bible in a year: 2 Samuel 11,12; Psalm 51

Tough justice

PREPARE
Two contrasting aspects of God's character are justice and mercy. How do you see these two characteristics working together? Which is predominant?

READ
1 Kings 2:26–46

EXPLORE
'Solomon, the man of peace, initially dealt mercifully with the rebels – Adonijah, Abiathar, Joab and Shimei (who had rebelled against David earlier). He agreed not to execute them, but imposed strict conditions on them – and everyone held their breath to see what would happen.

'Adonijah was the first to show his hand – it seems he still wanted the throne himself and thought he could undermine Solomon's authority if he "inherited" David's pretty young wife.

'Joab cracked next. He thought he could ignore all his past deceit and treachery and gain asylum by holding on to the Lord's altar.

'It looked for a while as if Shimei had settled down and accepted Solomon's terms, but then he broke the terms of his agreement with Solomon. Had he forgotten? Did he feel that he had served his time and could now do what he liked?

Did he feel that his personal situation was exempt from Solomon's conditions?

'Whatever the reasons that each one broke the terms of his conditions, Solomon showed he was ruthless in enforcing them. He was not going to make the same mistakes as his father in giving rebels enough room to cause more trouble!'

'But King Solomon will be blessed, and David's throne will remain secure before the LORD for ever.'
1 Kings 2:45

RESPOND
Solomon's behaviour here may seem very harsh, but God has always had an uncompromising attitude to sin. Praise the Lord that the punishment for your sin was born by Jesus at Calvary.

Bible in a year: 2 Samuel 13,14; 1 Corinthians 6

Friday 12 May
1 Kings 3:1–28

A wise and discerning heart

PREPARE
If God offered to give me anything I asked for, I wonder what I would choose: something material, something for someone else, a question answered, a relationship restored…

•••

READ
1 Kings 3:1–28

EXPLORE
'Today there was uproar in the court. Two women called on the king to decide which one owned a living baby and whose baby had accidentally been smothered in the night. At first, Solomon's suggestion seemed outrageous. He proposed cutting the live baby in half so that each woman could have an equal share! However, the women's reactions proved the king's wisdom. He knew that the real mother would fight for her child's life, whereas the other woman would reveal her deceit by her attitude.

'People have been commenting on Solomon's wisdom since his extravagant act of worship at Gibeon (he sacrificed a thousand offerings on that occasion!). The rumour is that God was pleased with his offering and offered to give Solomon whatever he wanted. Apparently, Solomon asked for God's help to rule his people (God's own people) wisely and well.

'Interesting, though… Despite Solomon's extravagant worship, and his increasingly noticeable wisdom in matters of state, he has recently made a marriage alliance with Pharaoh. I wonder what God thinks about that. Was it pragmatism or a lack of trust in God that motivated this decision?'

'So give your servant a discerning heart to govern your people and to distinguish between right and wrong.'
1 Kings 3:9

RESPOND
Wisdom is listening to God and doing what he says. James 1:5 encourages us to ask God for wisdom. Pray that God will increase your stock of his wisdom.

•••

Bible in a year: 2 Samuel 15,16; 1 Corinthians 7

Universal flourishing?

PREPARE
What do you picture when you hear a society is flourishing? Is it possible for every sector in society to be flourishing at the same time? How might we work towards a 'flourishing' in our own land?

READ
1 Kings 4:20–34

EXPLORE
'What a great time to be alive! Our nation is flourishing. Never before in our history have our borders extended so far, and our people been so settled – settled enough for every family to be able to invest in long-term agricultural projects, like vineyards and fig orchards, without the worry of war destroying everything.

'It is also a great time for careers – there are openings in the civil service and provincial administration department, the cavalry need ostlers, grooms and charioteers, and the royal kitchens are employing chefs of all kinds to prepare the mountain of food needed daily to provide for all those being fed in the royal palace. Meanwhile, the king himself has taken on a multitude of scribes to record his numerous songs, proverbs and observations of the kingdom's fauna and flora.

'Although everything, and everyone, seems to be thriving everywhere you look at this time, I did have occasion to pause and reflect when I met Adoniram in court. Apparently, he is the minister for forced labour and slavery (1 Kings 4:6). I wonder what all that is about?'

> The people of Judah and Israel were as numerous as the sand on the seashore; they ate, they drank and they were happy.
>
> **1 Kings 4:20**

RESPOND
Choose one brand that you buy regularly, and investigate how they treat their employees and the environment. How can your buying choices encourage universal flourishing?

Sunday 14 May
Psalm 93

King of kings for ever

PREPARE

'Majesty, worship his majesty: Unto Jesus be all glory honour and praise! Majesty, kingdom authority, flow from his throne...' (Jack Hayford, 1981).

....

READ
Psalm 93

EXPLORE

This week we have looked at David, the has-been king; Adonijah, the would-be king; and Solomon, the newly appointed king. All of them are poor reflections of the real King described in these verses – the King over all the world and everything in it.

God's throne is eternal – there need be no fights of succession. He is King, he always was King, and he always will be. That gives security to us and to all creation (vs 1,5) – God does not change laws on the basis of a whim or a mood. His laws are fair and will stand for ever.

God is all-powerful – he is clothed in majesty and armed with strength. He has the power to enforce his laws and to withstand any challenges to his authority. How would you define or picture majesty? What does God's majesty mean in your everyday living?

How often is the sea mentioned in this psalm? To the ancient Jews, the sea could symbolise chaos and destruction. It is powerful and uncontrollable, but before the might of God the King even the sea loses its power and is brought to worship (vs 3,4).

... the LORD on high is mighty. Your statutes, LORD, stand firm; holiness adorns your house for endless days.

Psalm 93:4b,5

RESPOND
What things in your life or in the world seem powerful, chaotic and destructive? Bring these to God, recognising that they are nothing before his great and mighty power. Praise God that he is King for ever and ever.

....

Bible in a year: 2 Samuel 19,20; 1 Corinthians 8

International cooperation

PREPARE
Think of any impressive buildings you have seen. The scale of Solomon's Temple was designed to be worthy of God's name. Let it help you praise his magnificence.

READ
1 Kings 5:1 – 6:10

EXPLORE

'I was chatting today with one of the older courtiers, who is excited about developments taking place at the moment. He told me that King David had wanted to build a Temple for the Lord and had laid in supplies of fine building materials, before God told him that it was his son who would build the Temple, not David himself. My friend is delighted to see Solomon embarking on that building project.

'It's typical of Solomon's wisdom that he has noted the strengths of different countries and has made a deal to make the most of these, trading Israeli agricultural products for Phoenician construction know-how. Usually, international agreements are bound by suspicion, mistrust and self-interest, but Solomon seems to have forged a close relationship with King Hiram that has sparked a blossoming of the forestry, quarrying and sea freight industries, and numerous training courses in all aspects of construction.

'Yet, with all the busy-ness, the city itself remains remarkably quiet. All the work dressing stones, shaping timber and beating metals is being done off-site. Even in construction this is a holy place!'

'I intend ... to build a temple for the Name of the LORD my God, as the LORD told my father David ... "Your son ... will build the temple for my Name."'

1 Kings 5:5

RESPOND
Solomon was clear that he was building the Temple to honour God's name. His dealings with Hiram caused Hiram to praise God. What things do you do to honour God's name or cause others to praise him?

Bible in a year: 2 Samuel 21,22; 1 Corinthians 9

Beautiful buildings

PREPARE
Reflect on these words from Proverbs: 'All a person's ways seem pure to them, but motives are weighed by the Lord' (Proverbs 16:2).

....

READ
1 Kings 6:11 – 7:12

EXPLORE
'Over the past seven years, the wonder of the Temple has been unfolding. Situated on top of Mount Moriah, and covered in gold, it is impossible for anyone visiting Jerusalem to miss it! Not only is the building itself spectacular from the outside, but all the interior walls and doors, even the most holy place, are made of the finest wood, carved exquisitely, and overlaid with gold.

'But the Temple is not the only building going up in Jerusalem – Solomon is also building himself a palace. The Temple is just about finished now, but the palace is only half done so far. The Temple is magnificent, but the palace is more than four times bigger! Because the Temple was being built to honour God's name, I thought it would be the grandest building in the world, but the palace is beginning to look quite amazing too.

'Of course, Solomon was making the Temple according to the dimensions God gave, whereas the palace is his own design. I suppose, as Israel becomes a bigger player in the world and we receive delegations from many foreign countries, we need an impressive palace to welcome them into – or do we?'

So Solomon built the temple and completed it ... It took Solomon thirteen years, however, to complete the construction of his palace.
1 Kings 6:14; 7:1

RESPOND
'Change my heart, O God ... may I be like you.
You are the potter, I am the clay,
Mould me and make me, this is what I pray.'*

---

*Eddie Espinosa, Mercy/Vineyard Publishing, 1982

....

Bible in a year: 2 Samuel 23,24; 1 Corinthians 10

Working for God

PREPARE
Henry Ford, the inventor and founder of Ford Motors, apparently said, 'Quality means doing it right, even if no one is looking.' What about our lives as Christians?

....

READ
1 Kings 7:13–51

EXPLORE
'I grew up knowing God was powerful and the controller of big things. He created the heavens and earth, he rolled back the Red Sea and he defeated the armies of Israel's enemies. But I am beginning to realise that God is also interested in detail…

'I was talking to Huram yesterday about the Temple furnishings. His workspace was dominated by an enormous waterlily-shaped basin, 5 metres across and 2 and a half metres deep. He had also used the waterlily design to shape the capitals for the tops of the pillars, and he was now busy creating fine bronze chains and hundreds of bronze pomegranates. These chains and pomegranates will decorate the capitals and will be 9 or 10 metres above our heads.

'I suggested it might be quicker and easier just to make bronze blobs rather than taking the trouble to make them look like pomegranates! No one would ever see them so high up. Huram explained that, first, he was following God's instructions and God had specified pomegranates; secondly, he was working for God, so it didn't matter what people thought – God could see the quality; and finally, his work was part of his worship to God and the expression of everything that he thought about God's greatness, beauty and holiness.'

Huram was filled with wisdom, with understanding and with knowledge to do all kinds of bronze work.

1 Kings 7:14

RESPOND
Read Ephesians 2:10, Colossians 3:17 and Colossians 3:23. Commit everything you have to do today to the Lord, praying that it honours him.

....

Bible in a year: 1 Kings 1,2; Psalm 55

Thursday 18 May

1 Kings 8:1–21

God's visible presence

PREPARE

'I will enter his gates with thanksgiving in my heart; I will enter his courts with praise.'*

. . . .

READ

1 Kings 8:1–21

EXPLORE

'Jerusalem is heaving with people, come to celebrate the Festival of Shelters, thanking God for the harvest and remembering our ancestors travelling through the wilderness. In every available space people have built shelters and there is a buzz of noise as the people cook, eat and sleep in their temporary "homes".

'Solomon decided to use this occasion to bring the Ark of the Covenant into its new permanent home. With crowds of people around, the king, the tribal chiefs and the heads of families followed the priests carrying the Ark into the Temple. All the available priests were making countless sacrifices to the Lord.

'The priests carried the Ark into the Most Holy Place and – as they withdrew – a cloud filled the whole Temple! Those of us watching in awe were reminded of the pillar of cloud, leading our ancestors through the wilderness. Could this

actually be God himself coming to inhabit his new home on earth?

'Solomon, inspired by this sign of God's presence, turned to the people and reminded them of the promises God has made to our nation. God has been faithful, keeping his promises. I can't imagine our nation ever being anything but faithful to God in return!'

'Praise be to the LORD, the God of Israel, who … has fulfilled what he promised with his own mouth to my father David.'

1 Kings 8:15

RESPOND

What promises has God made to you personally? Which have already been fulfilled, and which are you still waiting for? Praise God that he is trustworthy.

*Leona Von Brethorst, Maranatha! Music, 1976

. . . .

Bible in a year: 1 Kings 3–5; 1 Corinthians 11

Solomon's prayer

PREPARE
What specific things are you praying for your nation at the moment? How does it compare with what Solomon is praying?

....

READ
1 Kings 8:22–53

EXPLORE
'It's difficult today to imagine our nation ever being unfaithful to God, but as Solomon starts to pray, I realise (yet again) how much wiser he is!

'He knows how great God is and how high are the standards that God requires of those who follow him. He knows that covenants are two-way promises – God is keeping his part, but will our nation keep theirs? And Solomon knows that people's inclination is to turn away from God or to forget him.

'And so our wise king appeals to God's love and mercy. As he prays, Solomon imagines people falling out with neighbours and asks God for justice; he imagines foreigners coming to believe in our God and prays that they are welcomed. But above all, Solomon talks about our people sinning against the Lord, and imagines numerous disastrous scenarios resulting from that.

'On a day like today, when we are so conscious of God's presence with us, it's hard to believe that any of these scenarios could arise. But again and again the message is clear – if our nation then turns back to God, he will show mercy and forgive, and restore us in his love.'

> 'Yet give attention to your servant's prayer … LORD my God. Hear … the prayer that your servant is praying in your presence this day.'
> **1 Kings 8:28**

RESPOND
Pray for yourself and other believers that God will keep you faithful to him. Think of someone you know who has turned away from the Lord, and pray that they will return and ask for God's mercy and forgiveness.

....

Bible in a year: 1 Kings 6,7; 1 Corinthians 12

Saturday 20 May
1 Kings 8:54–66

God's blessing

PREPARE
How has God blessed you over the course of your life? Thank him for his care.

. . . .

READ
1 Kings 8:54–66

EXPLORE
'What an extraordinary festival it has been this year! Twice as long as usual to include the dedication of the Temple, along with our usual remembrance and thanksgiving (see Leviticus 23:33). Every sense was heightened – we heard many different accents and dialects around us, as vast numbers of people had travelled to Jerusalem from the far north to the far south of the country, and all places in between; we saw the pall of smoke over the city, and smelled the burning fat from the thousands of sacrifices taking place. And there was food everywhere, as people cooked and ate in their shelters, and shared with neighbours. What a joyous time it has been!

'On one occasion, Solomon stood up before the gathering of the people and blessed them. As he prayed, I was reminded of God's blessing of our patriarch, Abraham – God blessed him so that all peoples of the earth would be blessed through him (Genesis 12:2,3). Solomon prayed that God would bless Israel so that all other nations would know that he is the one and only God. It made me think – does blessing always carry purpose and responsibility with it? I feel very blessed with my position in court. I wonder how I should be sharing that blessing?

'... may he never leave us nor forsake us. May he turn our hearts to him, to walk in obedience to him...'

1 Kings 8:57b – 58a

RESPOND
What do you think about the purpose and responsibility of blessing? What more could you do, as an individual or together with your church, to share God's blessing with those around you?

. . . .

Bible in a year: 1 Kings 8,9; Psalms 56,57

God the Judge of the earth

PREPARE
Have a quick scan of some news headlines. What items in the news today challenge the idea of God being King and Judge of all the world?

. . . .

READ
Psalm 94

EXPLORE
This psalm is written in several sections as the psalmist wrestles with what he knows about God and what he sees in the world around him. He knows that God is the powerful King and Judge of the earth (vs 1–3) – so how can it be that evil flourishes (vs 4–7)? Even though evil people seem to be able to do what they like with God's people, and with the weak and vulnerable in society, the psalmist warns them that God knows what they are doing and will hold them to account (vs 8–15). But then the psalmist turns to fellow God-followers – it is not enough to sit back and wait for God to bring justice; we need to be actively working to deal with the injustice we see (v 16). And finally, the psalmist describes the security he finds in God, despite all the evil and injustice he sees and experiences (vs 17–23).

As you reflect on this psalm in the light of the world today, where are you in your thinking? Confused to see evil triumphing, confident that God will eventually bring justice, campaigning to make a difference or content in God's protection?

> But the Lord has become my fortress, and my God the rock in whom I take refuge.
>
> **Psalm 94:22**

RESPOND
Use the news headlines and this psalm to help you intercede that God's justice might prevail in our world. How is God challenging you to respond to the injustice you see?

. . . .

Bible in a year: 1 Kings 10,11; 1 Corinthians 13

Monday 22 May
1 Kings 9:1–28

Lukewarm!

PREPARE
'I know you inside and out, and find little to my liking. You're not cold, you're not hot – far better to be either cold or hot! You're stale. You're stagnant' (Revelation 3:15,16, *The Message*). How do these words challenge you?

....

READ
1 Kings 9:1–28

EXPLORE
'Solomon has been on the throne now for 24 years (see v 10 and 6:1).and I wonder if he is bored! He has been so rich and famous for so long, it must seem meaningless to him. He is still commissioning impressive building works, but without the enthusiasm he had for building the Temple. He is still worshipping God, but out of a sense of obligation. He still has a close partnership with King Hiram – jeopardised when he gave him some unproductive settlements. (Why was Solomon giving away some of the Lord's land anyway?) He had prayed for other nations to come to know our Lord, but his treatment of the indigenous people of Canaan would not have encouraged them to believe!

'No wonder the Lord reminded him of the example of his father David. David made huge mistakes – which Solomon doesn't

seem to be doing – but throughout his 40-year reign (in fact throughout his 70-year life) (2 Samuel 5:4), David was wholehearted in his love for and faithfulness to God. Apparently, God is not so impressed by the things we do. He is more concerned with our attitude to him.'

'... if you walk before me faithfully with integrity of heart and uprightness ... and do all I command ... I will establish your royal throne over Israel for ever...'
1 Kings 9:4,5a

RESPOND
How long have you been following the Lord? What could you do this week to deepen your relationship?

....

Bible in a year: 1 Kings 12,13; 1 Corinthians 14

Global fame

PREPARE
What gifts and talents has God given you? Pause to thank him for them and ask for opportunities to use them in his service.

READ
1 Kings 10:1–29

EXPLORE
'Undoubtedly, King Solomon is wise! His fame has spread all around the world and numerous foreign dignitaries (including the queen of Sheba) come to Jerusalem to learn from him. However, it seems that while they are learning godly wisdom from him, he is learning worldly wisdom from them.

'The foreigners who come praise God for the wisdom he has given Solomon, but it's a while since I have heard Solomon openly acknowledging that his wisdom, fame and wealth are gifts from the Lord. Instead, he seems to have become like other leaders in his display of wealth and power. Ivory thrones and gold shields are ostentatious with no practical purpose – except to impress our visitors!

'For years now, Israel has been experiencing its most peaceful era since our nation began, but our military forces are greater than they have ever been, with new garrison cities springing up. Maybe we are at peace because the armed forces are creating a deterrent which keeps other nations from attacking us.

'I am uneasy about all the trade taking place with Egypt and the personal wealth that Solomon is amassing (Deuteronomy 17:16,17). I wonder what God thinks?'

> The whole world sought audience with Solomon to hear the wisdom God had put in his heart.
>
> **1 Kings 10:24**

RESPOND
List some Christians in the public eye or in leadership positions. Pray that they will be able to keep God central in their lives.

Bible in a year: 1 Kings 14,15; 1 Corinthians 15

Foreign influences

PREPARE
Think of a good marriage you know. What do you observe that makes the relationship work well? Pray for God's blessing on marriages.

. . . .

READ
1 Kings 11:1–25

EXPLORE
'Another royal wedding today! Honestly, I can't keep up with them all – there have been hundreds. Solomon says he loves each wife (especially when speaking to the ambassador of their home country – listening to him, you would think each one was his favourite!). I don't know how he can keep up. I struggle to recognise them and remember their names.

'Each wife comes with her own culture and religion. Solomon says that part of making them welcome, and ensuring peace with their home countries, means that we need to have places for them to worship their own despicable "gods" – and so the building work continues. I've noticed too that Solomon doesn't just provide places for his wives to worship however they want; he even goes to the temples and offers sacrifices to these foreign deities. This is exactly what God warned us would happen if we married foreign women.

'Already we are starting to feel repercussions of God's displeasure towards our king. After more than a quarter of a century of peace, we now have rebel incursions attacking the country in the south and in the north-east. O Lord God, please protect us. Where will this end?'

As Solomon grew old, his wives turned his heart after other gods, and his heart was not fully devoted to the LORD his God, as the heart of David his father had been.

1 Kings 11:4

RESPOND
How do you put into practice Paul's warning in Colossians 4:5: 'Be wise in the way you act toward outsiders; make the most of every opportunity'?

. . . .

Bible in a year: 1 Kings 16,17; Psalms 58,59

The end of the era

PREPARE
Think back over your life so far. Can you see God's hand at work in coincidences, chance meetings and events that have later proved significant? Thank God for his work in your life.

....

READ
1 Kings 11:26–43

EXPLORE
'I write with a heavy heart today. King Solomon has died after 40 years on the throne, just like his father David. He was successful in many ways – raising our small nation up to become significant on the world stage, modernising and building impressive cities, increasing our wealth – but, sadly, he failed in the most important area. He did not follow the Lord wholeheartedly, but started worshipping false gods introduced by his many foreign wives.

'For now, his son Rehoboam has taken over as king, but everyone is waiting to see what happens next. God had told Solomon that the nation would split. For David's sake, a minority would stay with David's descendants, but the majority would be given to a new royal family.

'Solomon thought he had identified the person God had chosen to succeed him – Jeroboam, the leader of his labour force – and tried to kill him. Even at the end of his life, Solomon still hadn't realised that God is in control. For all his power, Solomon was not able to thwart God!'

… he said to Jeroboam, 'Take ten pieces for yourself, for this is what the LORD … says: "See, I am going to tear the kingdom out of Solomon's hand and give you ten tribes."'

1 Kings 11:31

RESPOND
Solomon's epitaph, for all his gifting and success, is that he was a failure. What would you like your epitaph to be? Pray, asking God to accomplish what he wills through you.

....

Bible in a year: 1 Kings 18,19; 1 Corinthians 16

Old Testament law

The first five books of the Bible – Genesis, Exodus, Leviticus, Numbers and Deuteronomy – are known by Jews as Torah, meaning 'instruction', 'teaching' or 'law'. However, a quick look at the five books shows that they are not all the same, and they are certainly not all lists of laws. Nevertheless, there are a *lot* of laws in them – more than 600 in fact!

The Ten Commandments

Perhaps not surprisingly, many people trying to read the Bible consecutively get bogged down when they get to Exodus 20, and often move on to an 'easier' part of the Bible. After reading about the origins of the world and humanity, the focus has narrowed to the story of one family and their escape from slavery in Egypt. Now the whole tone changes again as Moses hands down the first laws that God has revealed to him for his people: the Ten Commandments.

This was a turning point for them as they entered into a new covenant or contract with God (Exodus 24:7,8). Israel was now God's chosen people, which brought great privileges: he was present with them and committed to them. But, in turn, they were to live in a way that honoured him – holy God, holy people. Much of the rest of Exodus, Leviticus, Numbers and Deuteronomy is made up of these laws: instructions about how God wanted his people to live and worship him.

Reading Old Testament law

Reading laws is not a common practice for many of us, unless we are lawyers! So what should we do when we come to these sections of the Bible? Skim over them and move on? If we do, we will be missing out. As Paul said to Timothy, 'All Scripture is God-breathed and is useful for teaching, rebuking, correcting and training in righteousness' (2 Timothy 3:16). Here are some suggestions to help with reading and understanding God's laws.

Remember that the laws were given by God. So ask yourself, what does this reveal about the character of the one who gave the law? How might this help me in my quest to live a life that reflects him to the world?

The laws were given at a particular time in the Bible's story. God was equipping a new nation and he gave them these laws so that they would know what he wanted for them as his distinctive or holy people. They were not to be like the other nations (eg Leviticus 20:23; Deuteronomy 12:4). Many of the laws then were to mark them out as different from the nations around them.

God gave his people the laws for their own good. For example, many of the food laws were for the sake of health and hygiene in a hot climate with limited medical understanding (eg Leviticus 11). Sabbath and festivals gave a healthy rhythm to life, something we need as much as ever (eg Deuteronomy 16).

Knowing the law is not the same as keeping the law and interspersed with the laws are sections of narrative which demonstrate our inability to keep the law. The sacrificial laws are God's provision for restoration. Much later, Paul described the law as a guardian or schoolmaster to demonstrate to us our need of Jesus and bring us to him (Galatians 3:24).

Laws have different purposes. Some of the law is ceremonial, specifying how God should be worshipped in ways that honour him. Leviticus, for example, has a lot of detail about worship in the tabernacle, the portable meeting place. Other laws are civic laws.

Justice is a major theme in these laws. God's new society was to be a just society reflecting his own justice (eg Deuteronomy 15,19).

These laws were given to Israel in their particular cultural setting, which is different from ours. Some are impossible to keep even if we want to.

Jesus valued the law. He said that he had not come to abolish the law and the prophets, but to fulfil them (Matthew 5:17). He summarised it in this way:

'"Love the Lord your God with all your heart and with all your soul and with all your mind." This is the first and greatest commandment. And the second is like it: "Love your neighbour as yourself." All the Law and the Prophets hang on these two commandments' (Matthew 22:37–39).

Writer: Emlyn Williams

See also:
Gordon D Fee and Douglas Stuart, *How to Read the Bible for All Its Worth* (fourth edition), Zondervan, 2014
The Bible Project, *Biblical Law*, www.youtube.com/watch?v=Sew1kBIe-W0

THE RESTORATION STATION

Scripture Union

THE RESTORATION STATION TOOLBOX

THE RESTORATION STATION LOGBOOK

Use with **The Restoration Station** holiday club.

Includes photocopiable resources and **FREE** extras online

A BRAND-NEW HOLIDAY CLUB RESOURCE FROM SCRIPTURE UNION

At *The Restoration Station* children will be introduced to Jesus as a restorer. Using key stories from John's Gospel, the children will discover how Jesus is the master craftsman who heals and restores.

GET YOUR RESOURCES:
su.org.uk/therestorationstation

To be continued...

Acts is often described as a history of the early church. But forget dull, dusty schoolbooks. Acts is more like the *Indiana Jones* story on the New Testament shelf! Packed with arrests and escapes, storms and shipwrecks, impassioned speeches and miraculous signs, there is adventure at every turn.

About the writer
Cath Butler

Cath combines her work as a peripatetic music tutor with writing, spiritual direction and coordinating worship in her church. Her primary 'love languages' are the clarinet, pancakes, walks by the sea, reading, and journaling. She recently established @ PilgrimsPages – a new social media hub designed to help people explore journaling as a spiritual practice.

Luke penned its pages around AD 62, capturing the escapades of the apostles Peter (chapters 1–12) and Paul (chapters 13–28) as they spearhead the spread of the gospel 'in Jerusalem, and in all Judea and Samaria, and to the ends of the earth' (Acts 1:8).

The birth and expansion of the New Testament church were something like an ecclesiastical big bang, initiated by the giving of the Holy Spirit at Pentecost. This series focuses on the very first phase of that: the moments around the Spirit's outpouring and the subsequent witness in Jerusalem. As the title suggests, the story (itself a continuation of Luke's Gospel) continues both within Acts and beyond, right up to the era you and I occupy today. But the 'continuing' theme crops up in other ways too: each day we'll be exploring something the early church continued with or in – and that we can continue in too. So, see if you can trace the theme as it threads through our studies and, as you do, allow your own 'continuing' to be clarified, challenged, formed and shaped for the furthering of his kingdom.

Friday 26 May
Acts 1:1–11

Why wait?

PREPARE

What are you waiting for in this season? Take a moment to hold these things before God and invite him to meet you in the waiting.

. . . .

READ
Acts 1:1–11

EXPLORE

Whatever age we are, waiting – especially for something we expect to enjoy – can be incredibly hard. Like the disciples, so keen to see a kingdom of their own envisioning unveiled, we don't always understand what we're waiting for... or why it should be delayed. Thankfully, our times and transitions aren't in our hands (v 7), and the One who holds them has far greater plans and purposes than our own. His fulfilment of his promises is far better than our imperfect imaginings could ever be, his provision far more glorious.

Faced with the disciples' eager question (v 6), Jesus answers not with an ETA but with a course correction, expanding their horizons from national politics to global salvation (v 8). In doing so, he calls them to continue extending his kingdom and promises to equip them. I wonder if they had any idea just how much they'd need to overflow with the good gift of the Holy Spirit to carry out their commission.

For the disciples, waiting meant renewed purpose, receiving power and a deepening appreciation of God's agenda. How significant waiting can be in preparing us to continue our journey in partnership with him!

> ... while he was eating with them, he gave them this command: 'Do not leave Jerusalem, but wait for the gift my Father promised...'
>
> **Acts 1:4**

RESPOND

'Lord God, thank you that my times are in your hands. Please give me the grace to see your purposes in my waiting and fill me with expectation as you equip me for the way ahead.'

. . . .

Bible in a year: 1 Kings 20,21; 2 Corinthians 1

Take your place

PREPARE
'Lord Jesus, thank you that you have chosen me. With you, help me to play my part in your plans at this time and in this place.'

....

READ
Acts 1:12–26

EXPLORE
Fresh from Jesus' ascension, and fuelled by expectation of promise, it's no wonder this first prayer meeting flows unstoppably. Its other defining characteristic is its roll call: all are present, each one important. In particular, Luke lists 11 apostles by name, making the absence of the 12th even more conspicuous (v 13). The core of the new community of God's people is incomplete, one short of symbolising the 12 tribes of Israel. Yet Judas' difficult story isn't skimmed over; his deceit and death are understood as outworkings of God's word (vs 16–20). How ready are we to see God's hand even in seeming setbacks?

When it comes to filling Judas' place, one criterion outweighs all others: having been present, with the disciples and with Jesus, for the duration of his earthly ministry (v 21). Within this parameter, and submitted to God in prayer, lots are used for the last time in New Testament church governance (v 26). Leadership is vital and providing for its continuation is key: we must take our place. But whether we steer ourselves or spearhead global organisations, what matters most is that we are present with Jesus and his church.

> … Those present were Peter, John, James and Andrew; Philip and Thomas, Bartholomew and Matthew; James, son of Alphaeus and Simon the Zealot, and Judas son of James.
>
> **Acts 1:13**

RESPOND
Think about the areas where you lead. How you will prioritise time in the presence of Jesus so that your leadership flows from your discipleship?

....

Bible in a year: 1 Kings 22; Psalms 60,61

Sunday 28 May

Acts 2:1-13

Holy Spirit hallmarks

PREPARE
How have you experienced the Holy Spirit in your life so far? Dwell for a few moments on the most precious of these.

. . . .

READ
Acts 2:1-13

EXPLORE
A group of united disciples and a gathering of Jews for the harvest festival – this is the setting for the Holy Spirit's outpouring. Luke reaches for the legacy-rich symbols of wind and fire to picture for us the power, purity and very presence of God in the person of the Holy Spirit. Do you notice how the flame-like appearance separates to hover over the head of each disciple, and how the fire rests rather than ravages (v 3)? 'Our God is a consuming fire' (Hebrews 12:29), yet so personal and gentle in pouring his gifts and presence upon us.

Moving from filled to overflowing in a moment, the family of Jesus-followers is supernaturally enabled to speak of the wonders of God. Each is given a different expression – how beautiful that the Holy Spirit meets and ministers through each of us uniquely! Beyond natural comprehension and ability, bewildering (even offensive) to the international crowd of onlookers, the promised Spirit is the power they have been waiting for. The presence of God poured out personally and for all, mighty and yet gentle, perplexing and yet praise-inspiring in equal part – this gift is the power in which we, too, are to continue.

> They saw what seemed to be tongues of fire that separated and came to rest on each of them.
>
> **Acts 2:3**

RESPOND
How has the Holy Spirit enabled you to express the wonders of God? Thank him and ask for an opportunity to do so this week.

. . . .

Bible in a year: 2 Kings 1–3; 2 Corinthians 2

Beauty in between

PREPARE
'I can't believe this is finally happening!' What long-awaited, painstakingly prepared events have you been present for? How did it feel to be there?

READ
Acts 2:14–21

EXPLORE
Living 2,000 years later, it's hard for us to imagine how seismic Peter's explanation of events would have seemed to his audience of first-century Jews. Amazement, exhilaration, joy, awe, even fear – I'm sure a whole melting pot of emotions was present as they faced the first moments of a familiar prophecy being fulfilled. They were already surprised enough by what they saw and heard to suppose excessive alcohol consumption had been involved!

But Peter points to a passage from Joel (Joel 2:28–32) that foretold the start of a new age in the continuing story of salvation. It paints a picture of a time in which barriers of race, status, age and gender are removed, a time when the mind of God is made known as people prophesy in the power of the Spirit. It is a time when creation creaks in anticipation of Jesus' coming again, and a time when salvation is readily accessible to all who call on him. It's the time between the ascension and return of Jesus, and it is filled with the beauty of divisions reconciled, deepening revelation, and divine rescue. Best of all, we live through its continuing unfolding today!

'And everyone who calls on the name of the Lord will be saved.'

Acts 2:21

RESPOND
Which aspect of this in-between time do you most long to see manifest in and through your life – reconciliation, revelation or rescue? Ask God to fill you afresh with his Spirit so that you can continue his story of salvation.

Bible in a year: 2 Kings 4,5; 2 Corinthians 3

Tuesday 30 May
Acts 2:22–36

Proving the impossible

PREPARE
'God, where I encounter tensions as I explore and explain my faith, please give me the grace to know when to wrestle with and when to rest in your mysteries.'

READ
Acts 2:22–36

EXPLORE
Peter's sermon, the first recorded example of apostolic preaching in Acts, has one main purpose: to proclaim Jesus as 'Lord and Messiah' (v 36). As well as pointing to Jesus' miraculous ministry, Peter continues to appeal to the Old Testament, a scriptural authority accepted by his Jewish audience. Referencing the writings of King David, he highlights two passages that can only be understood from a prophetic point of view. The one who would not 'see decay', and who would sit at God's right hand (v 33) was not David personally, but his promised descendant, Jesus.

Far from purely academic, Peter's preaching packs plenty of punch. He confidently asserts God's sovereignty in Jesus' death and resurrection, while not absolving human participants – including his hearers – of their culpability (v 23). He confronts the human implausibility of defying the grave with the impossibility of deity being held by death (v 24). There is much to grapple with here: the interplay of God's plans, prophetic insight and human responsibility stretches our understanding significantly. Yet, weaving the strands together with eyewitness accounts, Peter explains the outpouring of the Spirit and proves the person of Christ (v 33). Calling people to an encounter with him – as challenging and exhilarating as it may be – is ours to continue in today.

'Therefore let all Israel be assured of this: God has made this Jesus, whom you crucified, both Lord and Messiah.'

Acts 2:36

RESPOND
Talk to Jesus about how you feel about introducing him to others. Why not ask for an opportunity to do so this week?

Bible in a year: 2 Kings 6,7; 2 Corinthians 4

Joy and generosity

PREPARE

Who is the most joyful person you know? What about the most generous? Thank God for each of them and pray that they will experience more of him.

....

READ

Acts 2:37–47

EXPLORE

The birth of the early church was explosive, but the literal heart of it was people who were ready to respond (v 37). Repentance, baptism and receiving the Spirit are closely linked in the New Testament. What stands out here is the expansive reach of Peter's heart and vision. His horizon for the fulfilment of the promised outpouring of the Spirit stretches well beyond those in front of him – to future generations and far-off people groups (v 39).

Like many things, an expansive heart starts at home. Luke's snapshot of life among the young community of believers highlights not just the practicalities but also the collective heart posture. Devotion and awe, compassion and generosity, gladness and sincerity – these all characterised the fledgling church. Overflowing in acts of worship and altruism, it's no wonder that the attractive nature of their common life found them favoured by the people. But perhaps the most important aspect of their fellowship was the simple fact that they were continuing together (v 44). What about us? Do we have hearts postured towards togetherness? Our highly individualistic culture makes it hard to reach for and realise that kind of community, but how potent it is in contrast.

Every day they continued to meet together in the temple courts. They broke bread in their homes and ate together with glad and sincere hearts.

Acts 2:46

RESPOND

'Lord God, form in me a heart that is turned towards joy and generosity, and give me hands that are quick to act upon its overflow.'

Bible in a year: 2 Kings 8,9; Psalms 62,63

Thursday 1 June
Acts 3:1–10

What do you see?

PREPARE
Paying attention to what we are paying attention to can be revealing. What have you been giving your attention to in the last hour, day and week? Pray from what you notice.

. . . .

READ
Acts 3:1–10

EXPLORE
Our story today starts comfortably in the realm of the ordinary: two pious Jews adhering to daily rhythms of devotion, and a lame man placed where he could ask for alms – just as he did every day. Extraordinary entered first through their eyes (vs 3,4). Their exchanged glances communicated expectation: the lame man's, of monetary help; Peter and John's, of heaven moving (v 5). Jesus' followers had seen the lame walk at his word on many occasions: freshly filled with his Spirit and power, why wouldn't they expect to continue his ministry?

Things get interesting when we allow ourselves to see the needs around us with eyes of expectant faith. We don't have to go out of our way: each ordinary day is crammed with opportunities to partner with God's extraordinary kingdom purposes, if only we will open our eyes to see. We may not always be able to provide what people think they need, but like Peter we know we have something so much better to offer (v 6). Life with Jesus is too good not to give freely, too amazing not to act upon and too incredible not to invite others into, where uncontainable joy abounds!

> Peter looked straight at him, as did John ... Then Peter said, 'Silver or gold I do not have, but what I do have I give you. In the name of Jesus Christ of Nazareth, walk.'
>
> **Acts 3:4,6**

RESPOND
Ask Jesus to give you eyes of expectation and show you opportunities for ministry today.

. . . .

Bible in a year: 2 Kings 10–12; 2 Corinthians 5

History and humility

PREPARE
Briefly sketch your immediate family tree, up to two generations behind and in front (as you are able). Next to each name, note a defining characteristic. Talk with God about the family traits you see.

READ
Acts 3:11–26

EXPLORE
Seizing a second moment of astonished curiosity, Peter addresses the crowd that converges on the scene of healing. Tracing through his confident claims and bold explanations, we find a couple of themes no less surprising to his hearers than the miracle they had just witnessed. Tucked away among the messianic terms he ascribes to Jesus is the title 'servant' (v 13) – a discreet reference to four songs in Isaiah that detail the suffering that God's chosen servant must undergo. Despite these prophecies, accepting a humble hero and a suffering servant as their Saviour was hard – and still can be today – especially as he invites us to imitate his ways.

The legacy we walk in is one of beautiful humility. It is also one of blessing for all humanity. In speaking of 'Abraham, Isaac and Jacob' (v 13), Peter appeals to the Jews' heritage, pointing them both to their long history and to the promised inheritance they looked for. Jesus is the fulfilment of that promise, their long-awaited blessing who, through them, brings refreshing to all peoples on earth (v 25). An inheritance of stunning humility; a history of incredible blessing: this is the legacy we continue to live in and from.

'The God of Abraham, Isaac and Jacob, the God of our fathers, has glorified his servant Jesus.'
Acts 3:13a

RESPOND
Holy Spirit, please increase your humility in me so that I might continue to bless those around me in the way Jesus did.

Bible in a year: 2 Kings 13,14; 2 Corinthians 6

Saturday 3 June

Acts 4:1–12

What's in a name?

PREPARE

What does your name mean? (Look it up online or ask a relative, if you're not sure!) How well does it fit who you are?

....

READ

Acts 4:1–12

EXPLORE

It didn't take long for the early church to upset the Jewish religious establishment. Whether the crowds that gathered could have provoked Roman fears of rebellion, or the assertions of the resurrection that ran contrary to Sadducean belief (v 2) – whatever the reason, the apostles found themselves in prison (v 3). On trial the next day, the one question aimed at them goes straight for the jugular: the source of their miraculous activity (v 7). Making a lame man walk was clearly beyond natural human capacity. What the religious leaders wanted to know was where the apostles' ability originated… and so they ask about the power, or the name, behind it.

Names are significant. In biblical times, someone's name encapsulated and communicated the fullness of their personhood; using their name invoked all that was true about them and employed all their authority. Acting in the name of Jesus brought the beauty of his heart, and all of heaven's powerful resources, into a broken earthly situation. His authority remains ours to continue using as we minister in his name today. How fully do you appreciate and avail yourself of that?

> They had Peter and John brought before them and began to question them: 'By what power or what name did you do this?'
>
> **Acts 4:7**

RESPOND

There is such richness and depth to discover in exploring Jesus' name. Meditate on his name this week, asking God to shape you as you do, so that you live more fully from his likeness and resources.

....

Bible in a year: 2 Kings 15,16; Psalms 64,65

Worship: hands and hearts

PREPARE
Look at your hands and imagine God holding you in his. Prayerfully offer him whatever thoughts and emotions surface as you do this.

∙∙

READ
Psalm 95

EXPLORE
Psalm 95 greets us with a riot of joyful song, thanksgiving and praise as we respond to the invitation to enter God's presence. I wonder how often we recognise worship – however it is expressed in our lives – as an invitation from God to enjoy his presence. As the psalm unfolds, we discover a clear focus: the God who is both Maker and Majesty, Creator and King. His unchanging and everlasting worth is the first, foremost and for ever foundation for our worship (vs 3–5). If that weren't enough, the psalmist reminds us that these heavenly hands that constructed worlds also cradle us. The One who made and owns us has also made himself ours, and this wonder both welcomes us into his heart and wells up within our own, overflowing as worship (vs 6,7).

His hands, our hearts: these are the places where true worship is forged. His hands are worthy. Are our hearts willing?

From the place where our desires, emotions, reason and will converge, we can choose between straying and striving or his paths and peace. Walking in his ways begins in wonder, is led by listening and ends in entering his rest – enjoying his presence eternally, both here and hereafter. What a breath-taking panorama of worship!

> ... for he is our God and we are the people of his pasture, the flock under his care.
>
> **Psalm 95:7**

RESPOND
'Lord God, you are worthy of all my worship. Please work within me a heart that is willing to walk in your ways – from here to eternity.'

∙∙

Bible in a year: 2 Kings 17,18; 2 Corinthians 7

Monday 5 June
Acts 4:13–22

Supernatural courage

PREPARE
What have you been known for in different times and places? In God's presence, make a list of qualities, roles and achievements, and ask for his perspective on them.

....

READ
Acts 4:13–22

EXPLORE
It was Peter and John's courage that marked them out (v 13). It spurred them through seismic shifts in the church's history, sustained them in powerful preaching and miraculous ministry and held them steady before amazed crowds and agitated religious rulers. Knowing that it didn't derive from education or anything innately remarkable about these men, the Jewish elite tentatively linked it to time with Jesus (v 13). They couldn't contradict such confidence, yet were reluctant to acknowledge its source, just as they couldn't refute that the lame man now leaped – yet refused to approve the spreading news (vs 16,17). What can *you* not deny, but struggle to support?

So when the two fearless apostles were threatened, their confidence in and allegiance to God would not be curtailed by critics too ready to capitulate to man (v 21). The Bible says much to endorse obeying earthly authorities, so long as that doesn't run counter to the revealed will of God. But the unwavering source of the apostles' continuing courage can be ours too. Let it be listening to God (v 19) that underpins both our confidence and our decisions.

> When they saw the courage of Peter and John and realised that they were unschooled, ordinary men, they were astonished and they took note that these men had been with Jesus.
>
> **Acts 4:13**

RESPOND
Who, what or where do you get your confidence from? Ask God to root your confidence in him so that you can live your life full of courage.

....

Bible in a year: 2 Kings 19,20; 2 Corinthians 8

More, please!

PREPARE
'God, as I come to your Word today, please pour out on me fresh passion to be part of seeing your kingdom come.'

....

READ
Acts 4:23–31

EXPLORE
Today we see the disciples continuing in prayer, continuing together, continuing to stand on the Scriptures, continuing to recognise both God's sovereignty and human responsibility behind events and continuing to acknowledge Jesus as God's humble Messiah. Far from dampening their spirits, the hostility they faced fuelled their passion to continue in what they'd been called to (v 29). How often do we pray for protection first – against opposition, rather than for fearlessness?

To continue in their mission and ministry, the new church community knew they needed more of God's enabling: more courage to speak, more miracles to attest their words and more of the authority of Jesus' name to be manifest. Asking for help is hard – perhaps pride gets in the way, or fear that our request will be rejected. But these believers didn't hesitate and God's answer was immediate and powerful. Of course he wanted them to have all they needed to continue in their commission: it was his plan and purpose they were partnering with, his glory and fame they sought to further! So, as soon as they asked, he poured out his Spirit afresh. Continuing to be filled, continuing to overflow – this constant rhythm of receiving God's life and running over with the courageous expression of it is available to us today!

'Now, Lord, consider their threats and enable your servants to speak your word with great boldness.'
Acts 4:29

RESPOND
Ask God for all you need to continue in what he has called you to, for his glory.

Bible in a year: 2 Kings 21,22; 2 Corinthians 9

WAY IN

Acts 4:32 – 8:3

Growth pains

Every step forward for the early church is accompanied by painful episodes that come at the church from both inside and outside. We rightly look back to these early days for examples of Christian community and courageous evangelism.

About the writer
Andy Bathgate

Andy retired as CEO of SU Scotland in March 2020 after 18 years in the role. He is married to Alyson and lives in Edinburgh where they are both involved in the leadership of their local church. They enjoy visiting art galleries, reading all kinds of books and looking after their three grandsons.

But that's not the whole story. Perfection is never claimed for these first Christians. As we'll see, growth produces a diverse community with troublesome members (5:1–11) and the clash of different backgrounds (6:1–7). How the church handles these challenges is fundamental to its development just as our managing of times of tension determines ours.

To describe the opposition faced by the new community of Jesus from the Sadducees and the Sanhedrin (5:17–42; 6:8–15; 7:54 – 8:3) as 'external' is only partly true. 'Friendly fire' might be a better description. The apostles see Jesus as the Jewish Messiah, the fulfilment of Israel's story. That's why we find them taking up residence in the Temple, initially working only within the Jewish community. The Jewish leaders find their claims about Jesus deeply offensive, and their rage makes Stephen the first Christian martyr.

God has always asked that we 'sing to the LORD, all the earth' (Psalm 96:1) and that 'all peoples see his glory' (Psalm 97:6), so the followers of Jesus will break free from the conception that this is a message only for Jews, demanding Jewish tradition and practices to be imposed on Gentiles. These chapters then form the launch pad for what will become a global mission.

What's mine is yours

PREPARE

'See what great love the Father has lavished on us' (1 John 3:1). Let the scope of God's love become an expression of gratitude as you pray now.

....

READ

Acts 4:32–37

EXPLORE

Before we owned a car, we had use of several, thanks to the generosity of church friends. One lady lent us her new car when she went on holiday, days after its purchase. For Luke, these kinds of action are marks of God's grace (v 33). A powerful work of grace may be evidenced by many coming to faith, but Luke associates it with every need in the Christian community being met (v 34), which of course becomes a witness to the world.

Some of the main signs of God's grace at work are unity (v 32) and generosity (vs 32,33). When God met Jacob at Bethel and Jesus befriended Zacchaeus (Genesis 28:22; Luke 19:8), the immediate result was a desire to give. In neither case was pressure exerted to elicit that response. Similarly, those in the early church who sold pieces of land or houses and gifted the proceeds seem to have done so freely and without coercion. Their laying of the money 'at the apostles' feet' says they were not dictating how the money should be used, as if their wealth gave them power to determine its allocation. Barnabas, who will play such a significant role in Acts (9:27; 11:22–26; and chapters 13–15) is introduced as a stand-out example, his integrity contrasting sharply with those in the next story (5:1–11).

All the believers were one in heart and mind. No one claimed that any of their possessions was their own, but they shared everything they had.

Acts 4:32

RESPOND

Are there any needy among your Christian community? What steps can you take to help?

....

Bible in a year: 2 Kings 23–25; Psalms 66,67

Thursday 8 June
Acts 5:1–11

The price paid

PREPARE
'Worship the LORD in the splendour of his holiness; tremble before him, all the earth' (Psalm 96:9). Take time to follow this command, beginning in silence and moving to open-hearted praise.

READ
Acts 5:1–11

EXPLORE
Two gifts are brought to God, both placed at the apostles' feet. But, as in the case of Cain and Abel, one gift is acceptable, the other questionable, and catastrophe ensues. Barnabas gave freely, holding nothing back. Ananias and Sapphira sold property but were under no obligation to give all the proceeds to the community (v 4). To pretend they were giving everything in a public show at the apostles' feet lacked integrity. That might seem a minor offence, but not in a community where 'behind its public affairs spiritual forces of incalculable power'* are operating. The deceit was not just fooling the church, it was opening a space for Satan to fill (v 3), lying to God (v 4), testing out the Spirit of the Lord (v 9). The future of the new Christian community was at stake. Would it be a place that took holiness seriously? A community where fear of offending God guided their every action?

Followers of Jesus are called to be perfect as their heavenly Father is perfect (Matthew 5:48), to root out sin and refuse it entry. A lackadaisical attitude to sin corrupts the whole community of believers. Adam and Eve's sin had a devastating effect on humanity. This story echoes that rebellion and warns of dire consequences.

> Great fear seized the whole church and all who heard about these events.
>
> **Acts 5:11**

RESPOND
'Without holiness no one will see the Lord' (Hebrews 12:14). Does that frighten or motivate you?

*James DG Dunn, *The Acts of the Apostles*, Eerdmans, 1996, p97

Bible in a year: 1 Chronicles 1–3; 2 Corinthians 10

The repair shop

PREPARE
How has God healed you? Give thanks for his work in your spirit, mind and body as he works to restore and transform you.

. . . .

READ
Acts 5:12–16

EXPLORE
The book of Acts is a continuation of what Jesus began, now working by his Spirit through the apostles. So, you would expect miracles. Jesus had told his disciples that they would do greater things than him (John 14:12), including more widespread miracles with many more people coming to know the Lord. So, no surprise that Luke reports a season flooded with miracles (so many that Peter doesn't have time to break his stride bringing healing to the crowds, v 15) with 'more and more' people becoming believers (v 14), the work spilling out of the Temple to the streets and countryside (vs 15,16).

These episodes immediately follow the tragedy of Ananias and Sapphira. Despite Satan's attempts to disrupt and divert Jesus' ongoing ministry, it flourishes, including Satan being cast out through exorcism of evil spirits (v 16). This brings us confidence but notice some still choose not to become followers of Jesus. People in the Temple are wary, perhaps suspicious of this new sect, perhaps fearful of the source of the miracles (v 13). Miracles create a buzz but do not always seal the deal: this was as true for Jesus as for the apostles (see John 6:26–40).

Nevertheless, more and more men and women believed in the Lord and were added to their number.

Acts 5:14

RESPOND
How do we see Jesus continuing his work today? What in your life and in that of your church are signs that he is at work? Give thanks and pray for more!

Bible in a year: 1 Chronicles 4–6; 2 Corinthians 11

Saturday 10 June
Acts 5:17–26

Green light

PREPARE

'God is working his purpose out as year succeeds to year' until the time when 'the earth will be filled with the glory of God.'* Lift praise to the One who cannot be defeated.

. . . .

READ
Acts 5:17–26

EXPLORE

Shakespeare described envy as 'the green sickness'.** But green also means 'go'. Both ideas appear in this story. The Sadducees, a wealthy, powerful group, assumed leadership positions in the Temple, many playing the role of Chief Priest or High Priest. The success of the Jesus movement was independent of them and consequently felt something of a threat, provoking them to jealousy (v 17). Few of us enjoy being out of control in something for which we feel responsible. Their response is to shut it down, having the apostles arrested and imprisoned.

It's another moment of peril for the emerging church. Will it survive this hostility from such a powerful opponent? As on countless other occasions in the history of the church, Jesus continues to build his church, ramming through the gates of hell (Matthew 16:18) that would seek to thwart it. An angel frees the apostles and gives them the green light to stand in the very place where opposition is fiercest and speak about new life in Christ (v 20). It's inexplicable to the Sanhedrin. They, like many world leaders since, are dumbfounded that the good news of Jesus cannot be chained. The good news will be taken to the ends of the earth.

'Go, stand in the temple courts,' he said, 'and tell the people all about this new life.'
Acts 5:20

RESPOND
Take time to pray for those in prison because of their commitment to Christ.

*From the hymn, 'God is working his purpose out' by Arthur Campbell Ainger, 1894
**Antony and Cleopatra, 3:2

. . . .

Bible in a year: 1 Chronicles 7–10; Psalm 68

Sing it loud

PREPARE
'What is your only comfort in life and death?'* Take some moments to frame your response.

. . . .

READ
Psalm 96

EXPLORE
Acts maps the transition of the community of Jesus from a Jewish heartland out to Gentile populations. This was not a foreign idea to earlier generations. Count the number of times the psalmist refers to '*all* the earth' or similar (vs 1,3,7,9,10,13). All nations or peoples are called to praise the Lord's name, and all stand accountable to him (vs 10,13). On the other side, God's people are mandated to 'proclaim his salvation' (v 2) and 'declare his glory' (v 3), to tell the nations 'The LORD reigns' (v 10). We too are never content with simply enjoying enrapturing worship as something internal to the Christian community. Our appreciation of the Lord must be declared globally.

Both singing and fear play a part in responding to God. There is true joy in singing to the Lord. The *new* song suggests a freshness in experience of God's marvellous deeds, in this case probably the witness of victory in battle. The singing reverberates throughout creation with heavens, sea, fields and trees rejoicing in jubilation. We can always find fresh reasons for rejoicing in the Lord as we explore his greatness. However, fear is also appropriate, even trembling, which gladly acknowledges that God is holy – unique among all other claims to deity, glorious, kingly and our judge. But even his judgement is a cause for rejoicing. It means that everything will be set right.

> For great is the LORD and most worthy of praise; he is to be feared above all gods.

Psalm 96:4

RESPOND
How does this psalm change your attitude to worship?

---

*The Heidelberg Catechism, Modern English version, 2011, Lord's Day 1

. . . .

Bible in a year: 1 Chronicles 11–14; 2 Corinthians 12

Acts 5:27–42

Unstoppable

PREPARE

The Bible places great emphasis on the name of Jesus (see vs 28,40,41). Reflect on the significance of his name, which means 'The Lord saves', and give thanks.

READ

Acts 5:27–42

EXPLORE

This is a passage of contrasts. Everywhere the story of Jesus is told some will accept it as good news while others will attempt to silence the witnesses. Opposition is at its most damaging and tragic when it emanates from those who claim religious faith. It is the Sanhedrin, the supreme council of the Jewish people, who call out the apostles for daring to challenge their prohibition (v 28). Their fury is deadly (v 33). But in contrast the apostles' teaching has 'filled Jerusalem' (v 28) as they teach 'day after day' (v 42). These contrasts are standard for Christian ministry.

The courage and determination of the apostles are impressive. They believe their message desperately needs to be heard. It's from and about what God has done (vs 29,30,31,32). It focuses on Jesus, whose resurrection and exaltation vindicate him as God's Messiah, sent to bring forgiveness and new life in the Spirit (vs 30–32). This remains the one message that can bring life and hope. Nothing can stop its advance. It takes the Pharisee Gamaliel (a positive view of a Pharisee!) to remind us that what is of God can never fail. None of that negates the pain of unwarranted flogging (v 40), although even that cannot dampen the sense of privilege in serving Jesus (v 41).

> Day after day, in the temple courts and from house to house, they never stopped teaching and proclaiming the good news that Jesus is the Messiah.
>
> **Acts 5:42**

RESPOND

What can we learn from the courage of the apostles? What difference will it make to your witness today?

Bible in a year: 1 Chronicles 15,16; 2 Corinthians 13

The joy of admin

PREPARE
Give thanks to God that his people are drawn from every tribe, language, people and nation (Revelation 5:9).

. . . .

READ
Acts 6:1–7

EXPLORE
The community of believers in Jesus was growing, despite opposition. But the challenges were not all external. Internal tensions were partly down to the success of the movement. The issue was not just about increasing numbers. It was the growing diversity of those who had come to believe in Jesus. Luke identifies two main groups: Hellenistic believers (Jewish incomers to Jerusalem who spoke Greek) and Hebraic believers (Hebrew or Aramaic speaking). Different languages reflect distinct cultures and can lead to misunderstanding but also potential favouritism. The Hellenists perceived discrimination in the treatment of widows in their group (v 1). They weren't getting their fair share of food. How would this complaint be dealt with? The unity of the believers depended on the answer.

The key leaders called a meeting that allowed everyone to be involved in determining the outcome. Seven people were affirmed as dependable, spiritually mature people to oversee the new system, allowing the apostles to concentrate on their calling. But, as we will see, roles were not tightly defined. Just as a church treasurer can engage in evangelism, so the seven stewards would also engage in defending and proclaiming the faith (Stephen in Acts 7; Philip in Acts 8). The issue was resolved and a united, focused group became ever more fruitful (v 7).

So the word of God spread. The number of disciples in Jerusalem increased rapidly, and a large number of priests became obedient to the faith.

Acts 6:7

RESPOND
Is anyone ignored or undervalued in your church? Ask God to help you recognise this and respond.

. . . .

Bible in a year: 1 Chronicles 17,18; Galatians 1

Wednesday 14 June

Acts 6:8–15

Fear and loathing

PREPARE

Give thanks for Christian martyrs, remaining faithful even to the point of death. They triumph over Satan through 'the blood of the Lamb and the word of their testimony' (Revelation 12:11).

....

READ

Acts 6:8–15

EXPLORE

Some of our negative responses result from feeling threatened. We fear change that may rob us of control or force us to admit we are wrong. Is that what produced the Jewish reaction to Stephen? He is painted as multi-talented but gracious, yet he provokes hostility. His arguments can't be refuted and that breeds false accusation and mob rule. It's all part of the cycle of opposition that Luke highlights in Acts (see 4:2–7; 5:11,17), only this time it will be deadly, as it remains for some now.

The apostles had done nothing to undermine the Temple. In fact, it was their go-to place for preaching to the crowds (5:12–14,19,20). But it was only Jesus, without the Temple, who could save. The Temple and the teaching of Moses were pointers to a coming Saviour, not the end point. Now, having fulfilled their function, they no longer had the status they once held. When God's Word comes to us, part of its job is to correct our wrong thinking (2 Timothy 3:16), especially when our views are somehow displacing Jesus. We don't always see when that's happening to us, and few enjoy having it pointed out.

Now Stephen, a man full of God's grace and power, performed great wonders and signs among the people.

Acts 6:8

RESPOND

Are there things in our church traditions or personal lives that we rely on more than Jesus? How can we be alert to this?

....

Bible in a year: 1 Chronicles 19–21; Psalm 69

Following the leader?

PREPARE

'Does he speak and then not act? Does he promise and not fulfil?' (Numbers 23:19b). Give thanks for God's trustworthiness.

....

READ
Acts 7:1–22

EXPLORE

Stephen stands accused of criticising the Temple and God's law (6:14). In answer, he tells a story, although its relevance is not immediately obvious! It's the story of God's promise and the people God chose to work it out on the ground – Abraham, Jacob, Joseph, Moses etc. The story involves hardship (slavery, famine, political treachery) and family animosity, along with some success (vs 10,17). There's migration but also rescue and return (vs 6,7), fulfilling God's promise and assuring us of his commitment to and protection of that promise. The Egyptians might try to kill off newborns, but God still raises up his next leader. Whatever the changes and challenges for the family of Abraham, God continues at work. It's the same for us. Our lives are not a random series of events. They have coherence because of God's promise to rescue us and bring us home to be with him.

Stephen asserts that God will work, whatever the obstacles. He builds a case throughout his speech that a major obstacle to God's purpose has been the almost universal rejection of God's chosen leaders by his own people. Joseph is his first example, jealousy (see Acts 5:17) inciting his brothers to get rid of him. They find themselves opposing their saviour!

'Leave your country and your people,' God said, 'and go to the land I will show you.'

Acts 7:3

RESPOND

Could jealousy prevent us seeing where God is at work? What else might blind us to this?

....

Bible in a year: 1 Chronicles 22,23; Galatians 2

Friday 16 June

Acts 7:23–43

Warts and all

PREPARE

'Though my father and mother forsake me, the LORD will receive me' (Psalm 27:10). Rejection is hard, but never our final destiny with God. Allow time to sense his acceptance of you.

. . . .

READ

Acts 7:23–43

EXPLORE

We could never accuse Stephen of hagiography. That's the term for biographies that erase anything negative about their subject. Stephen's warts-and-all presentation paints a picture of the Israelite nation as those who got it wrong, rejecting Moses (vs 35,39) and worshipping idols (vs 40,41,43). It's a sad story that underlines Stephen's thesis that the rejection of Jesus is part of a pattern. Despite God's commitment to his historic promise (v 32) and his raising up of Moses as a prophet and rescuer, the people shunned him. What was the exile to Babylon but a judgement on their blindness (v 43)? Jesus as the fulfilment of the promise of a prophet like Moses (v 37; Deuteronomy 18:15) suffers the same rebuff.

We could write our own history and that of the church in similar terms. *Bullies and Saints* is John Dickson's title for his honest look at the good and evil of Christian history.* Both are there, often confessing Jesus with lips but denying him in actions or lack of action. But the astounding truth is that all through the messiness of our history God is at work, patiently seeking to turn bullies into saints and deniers into 'repenters'.

> 'I am the God of your fathers, the God of Abraham, Isaac and Jacob.' Moses trembled with fear and did not dare to look.
>
> Acts 7:32

RESPOND

Let's not be too quick to criticise Stephen's detractors, but examine our own hearts to see where we might be ignoring what God is saying to us.

*John Dickson, Zondervan, 2021

. . . .

Bible in a year: 1 Chronicles 24–27; Galatians 3

The madness of crowds

PREPARE

Acts accentuates God's sovereignty in history (2:23; 3:13,18). Reflect on that in your life and that of your church.

. . . .

READ

Acts 7:44 – 8:3

EXPLORE

The climax of Stephen's speech seals his fate. He questions the Sanhedrin's understanding of the Temple and directly accuses them of resisting the Holy Spirit and failing to obey the law. He demonstrates that 'the relationship between God and his people predated the temple, the law and even the land of Israel'.* God appeared to people and was present with them, spoke and made promises to them, both within and outside the Promised Land – all before there was a moveable Temple/ tabernacle, far less the edifice in Jerusalem (vs 2–43). He even implies surprise that David, 'who enjoyed God's favour' (v 46), wasn't allowed to build the Temple: Solomon got the job. Then verses 49 and 50 clinch it – God can't be confined to any physical spot.

Stephen's conclusion? 'You are part of a long line of those who have missed the point and worst of all you've blanked Jesus.' This is a crunch point, a parting of ways between those who see Jesus as the fulfilment of Israel's history and those who see a blasphemer whose faction must be violently counteracted. Stephen's death echoes his Lord's, with Saul an approving bystander, and a pogrom against Jewish believers in Jesus ensues (8:1–3).

> But Stephen, full of the Holy Spirit, looked up to heaven and saw the glory of God, and Jesus standing at the right hand of God.
>
> **Acts 7:55**

RESPOND

Compare Stephen and members of the Sanhedrin. Who has most to teach us? Make a list of lessons we can learn from both and give thanks for all we have gained by Stephen's courageous stand.

*Conrad Gempf, 'Acts of the Apostles', in *The New Bible Commentary, 21st Century Edition*, IVP, 1994

. . . .

Bible in a year: 1 Chronicles 28,29; Psalms 70,71

Sunday 18 June
Psalm 97

Far above all

PREPARE

'Just and true are your ways, King of the nations' (Revelation 15:3b). Repeat these words in prayer, adding examples of where you have known this to be true.

. . . .

READ
Psalm 97

EXPLORE

'I hope he's burning in hell': words spoken by a grieving mother, directed at her 21-year-old son's murderer. We don't know if she believed in hell, but either way her words express a human reaction. It's a cry against injustice and for things to be put right; for people to be held to account for evil. Psalm 97 addresses this sensitive area, proclaiming God as the King who consumes his foes (v 3) and puts idol worshippers to shame (v 7). This is a cause for gladness because we hate evil and need to be guarded from its attacks (v 10). We believe evil will be brought to its knees. The God before whom even Everest and Kilimanjaro melt will see to it (v 5).

We rejoice in God's righteousness, awaiting the day when it becomes clear to all that Christ is 'the beginning and the firstborn' (Colossians 1:18). This is not a cause for smugness, complacency or being revengeful. Rather we share God's foundational commitment to righteousness and justice and resultant hatred of evil. We rejoice when right is done and weep when it is not. It means keeping our hearts right and warning those who think themselves unaccountable. But ultimately it makes us optimistic, hopeful, joyful people.

Let those who love the LORD hate evil, for he guards the lives of his faithful ones and delivers them from the hand of the wicked.

Psalm 97:10

RESPOND
How do you (corporately as well as individually) express your love for justice and your hatred of evil?

. . . .

Bible in a year: 2 Chronicles 1,2; Galatians 4

Scripture Union

By purchasing *Daily Bread*, you are helping to support Scripture Union's mission with children and young people. Thank you!

Subscribe to our free supporter and prayer magazine at su.org.uk/ connectingyou

WAY IN

Acts 8:4 – 12:19a

Growth against the odds

These chapters describe the early church growing in the face of opposition. It was an exciting but challenging time. The persecution recorded at the start of our readings took place shortly after

About the writer
John Grayston

Now retired after 37 years on the Scripture Union staff, John still writes, teaches and preaches. He is on the leadership team at Tile Kiln Church in Chelmsford. When he can he escapes to his allotment, or the mountains, walking or skiing with his wife Jenny. He has two children and seven grandchildren.

Jesus' death and resurrection (probably around AD 33). Paul's meeting with the risen Jesus likely took place in AD 34. Dates after that are difficult to identify until the death of Herod in AD 44. (This is not Herod the Great who killed the babies in Bethlehem, nor Herod Antipas who ruled Galilee during the time of Jesus' ministry, but Herod Agrippa, Herod the Great's grandson.) This suggests that the execution of James and the imprisonment of Peter took place in AD 43.

Luke selects his material carefully, concentrating on specific episodes. He emphasises the powerful activity of God through the Holy Spirit. He shows ordinary people telling others about Jesus. He demonstrates that the good news of Jesus was for all people – Jews and non-Jews. To us this may not seem a big issue, but it was a key truth that the early church struggled to learn. There is an honesty in the way he recounts the events; the early Christians have weaknesses but are still used by God.

Despite the differences in our context and circumstances, there is much that we can learn from these chapters. Be encouraged by the way that God's power is displayed through his people. Be challenged by the welcome that God offers to all. Believe that God is still building his church.

The word is out

PREPARE
Recall a time when you spoke to someone about Jesus. What was the response? How did you feel?

. . . .

READ
Acts 8:4–25

EXPLORE
The early Christians are facing opposition. They are effectively refugees on the move. How might we expect them to behave? Keep a low profile? Stay quiet for a bit? Well, those might be natural and logical responses. But it's not what we see here. As they are dispersed, they still talk about what Jesus has done for them. Often in the history of the church, opposition has led to growth.

The opposition of the Jewish leaders, and sometimes the Roman authorities, is part of a spiritual battle. Sometimes that battle can take more subtle forms. Today we may be confronted by apathy rather than overt opposition. Simon wants spiritual power, but for his own purposes and to boost his personal status. But God cannot be manipulated in this or any other way. The gift of the Spirit, promised to all who believe and given to these new believers in Samaria through the laying on of the apostles' hands (v 17), is the free gift of God. It cannot be bought or earned. We simply have to trust and be open, knowing that it is the Spirit who gives us the power to speak about Jesus and to face the spiritual battle.

Those who had been scattered preached the word wherever they went.

Acts 8:4

RESPOND
Is there anyone with whom you could talk about Jesus this week? Pray for an opportunity to share your faith and witness to Jesus. Ask God to help you through the Spirit.

. . . .

Bible in a year: 2 Chronicles 3–5; Galatians 5

Tuesday 20 June

Acts 8:26–40

Brief encounter

PREPARE

Thank God for the power of the Bible to speak. Pray that it will speak to you today.

....

READ

Acts 8:26–40

EXPLORE

Things are going well. God is working. Then suddenly God tells you to go to a remote desert road. All rather unexpected. Philip was one of the seven appointed to help the apostles administer aid (6:1–7); here he is in a mini-revival and being asked to leave it with no reason given. We won't always understand what God is doing, but we can trust him. What matters is obedience, even when we can't see where it will lead.

Philip goes – and an amazing encounter results. This Ethiopian official worshipped God and was serious enough to make the trip to Jerusalem but had not fully converted to Judaism. Reading from Isaiah 53, he is puzzled and needs Philip to explain that centuries earlier Isaiah had been writing about Jesus. That centuries earlier, God had been preparing the way. That Jesus has suffered in our place. That Jesus was rejected so that we might be accepted.

We are unlikely to bump into Ethiopians reading Isaiah in a chariot. But we will meet people in whom the Holy Spirit is at work, preparing them to hear the good news of Jesus. How ready are we to be used by God as Philip was? We may be surprised at the response.

> Then Philip began with that very passage of Scripture and told him the good news about Jesus.
>
> **Acts 8:35**

RESPOND

Pray for a sensitivity to what the Spirit is doing in people you meet.

....

Bible in a year: 2 Chronicles 6,7; Galatians 6

About turn

PREPARE
Think about your journey of faith. Maybe you had a sudden life-changing experience of Jesus. Maybe it was a gradual process. Maybe you can't remember a time when you didn't know Jesus. Whatever form it took, thank him for it.

READ
Acts 9:1–19a

EXPLORE
These verses are normally referred to as 'Paul's conversion'. They are headed that way in many Bibles. But we need to be careful. Paul is not converted from something to something else. As he meets the risen Lord Jesus, he comes to realise that Jesus is the true fulfilment of all that he had believed up to this point, that all God's plans, all the promises of the Old Testament and his Jewish convictions, are completed in Jesus.

His blinding and the subsequent restoration of his sight sum it up. He now sees things in a new way; the light has dawned. He can now see the truth. It involves a dramatic change. We meet Jesus in different ways but there will always be change. For some there may be a definite moment when the light dawns; for others it may be a series of small steps. There may be a real sense of turning from one set of beliefs to the truth we find in Jesus. The key thing is that we meet the risen Jesus. We will experience life in a new way. We will learn to live differently. We have a new Master and a new purpose. We are no longer the people we were.

Then Ananias … said, 'Brother Saul, the Lord – Jesus, who appeared to you on the road as you were coming here – has sent me so that you may see again and be filled with the Holy Spirit.'

Acts 9:17

RESPOND
Pray that non-Christian friends may see the light.

Bible in a year: 2 Chronicles 8,9; Psalm 72

Thursday 22 June

Acts 9:19b–31

Peace-making

PREPARE

Sit quietly for a few moments and allow God to speak to you of his presence and his power.

....

READ

Acts 9:19b–31

EXPLORE

I visited an eastern European country a few months after the end of the Communist regime to work with an emerging Scripture Union movement, travelling across the country with a Lutheran minister. Eighteen months later I returned. Preaching in a church of a different denomination, I was surprised and moved to find him in the congregation. He told me that it was the first time he had worshipped in a congregation other than his own, explaining that any stranger was a potential government agent.

The church in Jerusalem felt much the same about Paul. Despite his eloquent and powerful arguments that Jesus was the Son of God (v 20) and the promised Messiah (v 22), they could not forget that he was the one who had so violently persecuted them. Their fear and suspicion were perfectly natural. But maybe they doubted the power of God to change even the most hardened opponent.

Church is not always easy. There will sometimes be misunderstanding, tension and disagreement. New people may not always fit in. This is why we need people like Barnabas (v 27): gentle, compassionate people. People with the wisdom and the sensitivity to see what God is doing and to speak out. People who see the best in others.

> ... he tried to join the disciples, but they were all afraid of him, not believing that he really was a disciple. But Barnabas took him and brought him to the apostles ...

Acts 9:26,27

RESPOND

Pray for your church and especially for any areas of tension. Pray for more people like Barnabas. Pray that you may be a peacemaker.

....

Bible in a year: 2 Chronicles 10–12; Ephesians 1

Roles for all

PREPARE
Think of those who have helped you in some way in your Christian life. Let the memory encourage you as you read.

....

READ
Acts 9:32–43

EXPLORE
I am sometimes puzzled when I read these accounts of the early church. Why don't we see God working like this today? We *do* see God working; people *are* healed; they come to faith and they grow in faith. But it all seems rather different from the days of the early church. But even then, not everyone was healed (see, for example, 2 Timothy 4:20). God's power has not changed, but he chooses when, where and how that power is exercised. We can and should pray confidently and expectantly for God to act but cannot dictate to him. Perhaps there are key times in the history of the church when God acts in special ways. But he is always at work, and we can always trust him – just as Peter does here.

Widows seem to have had a special place in the early church. Being vulnerable they were supported, but they also had a ministry (vs 39,41). Ministry in the early church seems to have involved everyone. Are there some in our churches who are excluded from ministry on the basis of age, gender or ethnicity? God works not just in signs and wonders but in quiet acts of Christian service sometimes done by unlikely people.

> 'Aeneas,' Peter said to him, 'Jesus Christ heals you. Get up and roll up your mat.' Immediately Aeneas got up.
>
> **Acts 9:34**

RESPOND
How can we incorporate everyone in the life and mission of our church and ensure that all have a ministry appropriate to their gifts, skills and experience?

....

Bible in a year: 2 Chronicles 13–15; Ephesians 2

Saturday 24 June

Acts 10:1–16

A tale of two people

PREPARE

Ask God to show you something fresh today, to deepen your understanding of his purposes for your life.

....

READ

Acts 10:1–16

EXPLORE

God is preparing two men for a meeting which will shape the future of the church. We find it hard to understand why the first Jewish Christians found it so difficult to accept that non-Jews (Gentiles) could be full members of God's church. The Old Testament made it clear that God's plan was for the nations (eg Genesis 12:1–3; Isaiah 42:1). Jesus had told his disciples to go to all nations (Matthew 28:19). But steeped in the traditions of Judaism and the expectation of a Messiah who would deliver them *from* the nations, it was far harder than we might think. The need to break down the dividing wall between Jew and Gentile is a common theme in the New Testament.

So in preparation for the visit of the messengers from Cornelius – who is being prepared in his own way – Peter has to be gently prepared with this rather strange vision. The heart of it is that God does not make the distinctions we do. We shall see how the story plays out next week and will look at the implications for the church today. For now, let's hold on to the need to listen to God even when we don't fully understand. None of us has complete understanding, and God moves us on in unexpected ways.

> The voice spoke to him a second time, 'Do not call anything impure that God has made clean.'
>
> **Acts 10:15**

RESPOND

Take some time this weekend to be quiet and listen to God. Ask him what he wants to say to you.

....

Bible in a year: 2 Chronicles 16,17; Psalm 73

Celebrate salvation

PREPARE
Look back over your life with God. Identify key moments when you have experienced his love. As you read the psalm, let it lead you into praise.

....

READ
Psalm 98

EXPLORE
Here is a glorious, enthusiastic celebration of all that God has done for his people. Perhaps the psalmist is thinking of the Exodus, or the return from exile, or victory in battle. Whatever it was, God had saved his people. Look through the psalm again to see some of the ways in which the writer describes God and his actions.

We have even more to celebrate. No doubt Paul, having met the crucified and risen Christ, could have used words like this to describe his experience. You could check out some of his own words in Romans 11:33–36 or Colossians 1:15–20. So, what better psalm to read on this first day of the week when we gather to celebrate the death and resurrection of Jesus – God's supreme victory over all the powers of evil.

The praise here is exuberant and abandoned: shouting, singing, making music. The whole of creation joining in. We may express our feelings in different ways, depending on our mood, our personality or the nature of worship in our churches. The key thing is to focus on who God is, what he has done for us and to respond in ways that genuinely celebrate his character and our gratitude and that honour him.

Sing to the LORD a new song, for he has done marvellous things; his right hand and his holy arm have worked salvation for him.

Psalm 98:1

RESPOND
Look for things to praise God for today. Pick up some of the ideas in this psalm to express them. Praise him.

....

Bible in a year: 2 Chronicles 18–20; Ephesians 3

Monday 26 June
Acts 10:17–33

All welcome

PREPARE
Pray that as you read you may be prepared to see things from a different perspective.

....

READ
Acts 10:17–33

EXPLORE
If you are anything like me there will be times when you know something but find it hard to put it into practice. Peter is in a similar position. The vision had started him thinking, but now he has to work it out. There is a lot at stake. He is being called to do something that goes against everything he believes. He knows he will face criticism from others. Nevertheless, he is obedient to God's call without knowing exactly where it will lead. That requires a lot of faith. Sometimes we will have to step out not knowing where it will end but trusting God to work out his purposes.

Peter is discovering that the old divisions have gone. A careful reading of the Old Testament would have told him that God's promise was to bless all nations through Abraham's descendants (Genesis 12:1–3), that the stranger was to be welcomed and accepted (Leviticus 19:34; Numbers 9:14). God's love extends to the whole world (John 3:16).

We humans have a natural tendency to erect barriers. To exclude those who are not like us. Any such barriers, based on things like age, social standing or ethnic origin, have no place in the life or mission of the church.

> 'But God has shown me that I should not call anyone impure or unclean. So when I was sent for, I came without raising any objection. May I ask why you sent for me?'
>
> **Acts 10:28,29**

RESPOND
Where do we put up walls that exclude some people? What might make people feel uncomfortable or unwelcome in your church? Pray that your church will always extend a welcome to all.

....

Bible in a year: 2 Chronicles 21–23; Ephesians 4

Tell it like it is

PREPARE
Thank God for the work of his Spirit in your life. Pray that he will continue to lead you into truth (John 16:13).

....

READ
Acts 10:34–48

EXPLORE
For many years I have spoken on Christian holidays. In our evening meetings a testimony by a cook, a caretaker or a ski instructor can have just as much impact as my Bible talk. A testimony speaks from personal experience. It tells a story of something that has been lived. Jesus told his followers that they would be witnesses (Acts 1:8), telling the story of all that they had seen, heard and experienced of Jesus, his life, his death and resurrection. Just as Peter does here.

Our experience of Jesus will be very different from Peter's. We have not walked the dusty roads of Galilee with him. But we have known his love, have felt his closeness, have seen him answer prayer. Our story will feature some of the elements of Peter's story. Look back to see what he says about Jesus. At its heart is Jesus' death and resurrection. That will be the focus of our story too.

It is not down to us to make people followers of Jesus. We share our experience of Jesus; the rest is down to God and the work of his Spirit – just as happens here (vs 44–48). Trust him to be at work.

While Peter was still speaking these words, the Holy Spirit came on all who heard the message.

Acts 10:44

RESPOND
Think about the key elements of your own story. Rehearse it in your mind so that when someone asks, you can tell it simply and clearly.

....

Bible in a year: 2 Chronicles 24,25; Ephesians 5

Wednesday 28 June
Acts 11:1–18

All change

PREPARE

Recall times when the way that you see things has changed. Thank God for the way that his Spirit leads. Pray that you may be open to further change.

....

READ
Acts 11:1–18

EXPLORE

Peter may have got there, but some of the leaders in Jerusalem hadn't. Peter no doubt expected criticism about his time in Caesarea – and he got it (v 2). Old habits and old understandings die hard. But listening to what God had done, these leaders see that change is coming. It would be easy from our perspective to criticise them – and in his letters Paul has quite a bit to say about those who refused to change their way of thinking – but how often do we stick with our own attitudes even when God is calling us to change?

We could benefit from cultivating the attitude here. *Keep an open mind.* There is always the possibility that the way we have always seen things may be wrong or that God may be doing something new. *Listen carefully.* Rather than dismissing Peter, they listen to his account. When we disagree, listening to others is important. *Look at what God is doing.* If that goes against what we think, then we may have to change. *Have a big heart.* They didn't like what was happening, but they saw it as God's doing and praised him. Let's be generous even when things don't go the way we would like.

> When they heard this, they had no further objections and praised God, saying, 'So then, even to Gentiles God has granted repentance that leads to life.'
>
> **Acts 11:18**

RESPOND

Are there changes happening in your church life that you find hard? Pray that God will help you to see the right way forward.

....

Bible in a year: 2 Chronicles 26–28; Psalm 74

Generosity in action

PREPARE
Pause to recall all that God has done for you. Thank him and be ready to receive more from him.

. . . .

READ
Acts 11:19–30

EXPLORE
Scattered by persecution, the priority of the early followers of Jesus is still bringing the good news to Jews. However, some go to Antioch and start telling non-Jews, which leads to the same sort of reaction as we saw yesterday: part suspicion, part openness to what God is doing.

Barnabas ensures that the new Christians are encouraged and properly taught. This brings Paul back into play. Barnabas has seen Paul's teaching gift and, now that Paul has spent time reflecting and meeting with God, he is better able to teach others. We need to know what we believe if we are to share our faith.

The practical help provided by the new Christians in Antioch to the church in Jerusalem helps to build bridges. There is a generosity of spirit shown by Barnabas in his dealings with the church in Antioch and with Paul. There is a generosity of spirit shown by the church in Antioch reaching out to the church in Judea (vs 29,30). We are to be marked by a generosity which welcomes and accepts others (Romans 15:7) and which meets the practical needs of others (2 Corinthians 8:1–9). In both cases this is a natural response to what God has done for us.

> Barnabas went to Tarsus to look for Saul … he brought him to Antioch. So for a whole year Barnabas and Saul met with the church and taught great numbers of people.
>
> **Acts 11:25,26**

RESPOND
Where might you need to show generosity of spirit? Is there someone who needs a special welcome, or practical help? Pray, and resolve to do something.

. . . .

Bible in a year: 2 Chronicles 29,30; Ephesians 6

Friday 30 June
Acts 12:1–19a

The great escape

PREPARE

Give God any doubts and fears you have. Look for his reassurance.

....

READ

Acts 12:1–19a

EXPLORE

As I write, war rages in Ukraine – and it is far from the only conflict in the world. Human history is littered with power-hungry tyrants who inflict pain on their own people and on others. The Roman Empire in which the early church grew had its share. Emperors were in supreme control and were often harsh, but there were also local puppet rulers who could be violent and oppressive. Herod was one such. Seeking personal popularity and status, he decided to persecute the church and had James executed.

James is killed. Peter is released. Why should this be? We don't know. God is in control and his decisions may not always make sense to us, but we know from Hebrews 11 that faith can be demonstrated both in release and in suffering (Hebrews 11:32–38). Peter's faith doesn't seem that strong – he thinks it is all a dream (v 9). The faith of the others, praying earnestly for his release (v 5), but telling Rhoda she is out of her mind when she reports that Peter is at the door (v 15), seems even weaker. Faith and doubt can coexist. Most of us have doubts from time to time. Faced honestly in prayer and with support from others they can strengthen our faith.

> Then Peter came to himself and said, 'Now I know without a doubt that the Lord has sent his angel and rescued me from Herod's clutches...'
>
> **Acts 12:11**

RESPOND

Opposition to Christian faith can take many forms. For some, it takes the form of violent persecution, imprisonment, removal of rights, even death. Pray today for fellow Christians facing such opposition.

....

Bible in a year: 2 Chronicles 31,32; Luke 1:1–38